Gran Torino

Study Guide

by
Ingrid Stritzelberger

Diesterweg
westermann

NEUSPRACHLICHE BIBLIOTHEK

Gran Torino

Study Guide
by Ingrid Stritzelberger

> *"We may have all come on different ships, but we're in the same boat now."*
>
> (Martin Luther King Jr.)

westermann GRUPPE

© 2018 Bildungshaus Schulbuchverlage
Westermann Schroedel Diesterweg
Schöningh Winklers GmbH, Braunschweig
www.diesterweg.de

Druck A[1] / Jahr 2018
Alle Drucke der Serie A sind im Unterricht parallel verwendbar.

Redaktion: Ingrid Stritzelberger, Denkendorf und Jenny Poole, Waiblingen
Umschlagfoto: © Alberto E. Rodriguez / Getty Images, München
Layout: Harald Thumser, Frankfurt am Main
Satz: Satz und Grafik Walter Laß e. K., Meitingen
Druck und Bindung: westermann druck GmbH, Braunschweig

ISBN 978-3-425-**04996**-0

Table of Contents

Introduction

Gran Torino (USA 2008, 112 minutes) is embedded in the unit which deals with people's identity. The film offers the example of the Hmong. Do they belong? To which group do they belong? How would they present themselves: as Asian-Americans, as Hmong-Americans, as Americans? Or do they feel ambiguous about their identity because they have not yet found their place?

Today, the majority of Americans trace their family origins to a country other than the United States. The same goes for the protagonists. Both, Walt and his family as well as his Hmong neighbours, are immigrants to the US. Whereas Walt came from Poland in the search of better opportunities, the Hmong came to America for political reasons, as a consequence of the Vietnam War. Fighting on the side of the Americans, they could not stay on after the American withdrawal in 1975.

They are neighbours in a changing suburban America, an America which has been characterised by President Jimmy Carter like this: "We become not a melting pot but a beautiful mosaic. Different people, different beliefs, different yearnings, different hopes, different dreams." That is his way of summarising the "salad bowl", "pizza", "quilt" and "melting pot" images.

Global issues that lead to immigration and refugees will have to be dealt with to understand the topics of Identity and Belonging.

In order to do this, Pre-viewing II proposes group work material on the American Dream, seen through the eyes of men fighting for America in Korea and in Vietnam, of people from Southeast Asia fleeing to America and of Hmong settling in America.

An extensive Immigration Timeline includes important facts and figures as well as relevant immigration laws. With statistics and graphs, as well as a cartoon, students will be able to talk about immigration and discuss questions like:
What obligations, if any, do nations have towards refugees?
What obligation does the United States have to people, such as the Hmong, who fight alongside the U.S. in its foreign wars?
What challenges do immigrants face in starting new lives for themselves?

Another interesting method of acquainting the class with the foreign politics history of the U.S. after WW II are three-minute talks:
Teams of students prepare short talks on topics like: The Truman Doctrine and the Marshall Plan, The Korean War, The Bay of Pigs Invasion, The Cuban Missile Crisis, The Vietnam War, The Iraq-Iran War (1980-1988), The Gulf War (1990-91), 9/11 and George W. Bush's War on Terror.
They do not use any other visualization apart from maps (no Powerpoint); the focus is on speaking and listening; it serves as preparation for communication exams.

Relevant photos and maps on political issues are also included in the Pre-viewing section, as well as photos of two vintage cars – a Gran Torino and a Mercedes-Benz Coupé – so that students can discuss what makes people desire and cherish vintage cars.

Pre-viewing Activities I

Worksheet   Vintage Cars

Tasks:

Briefly describe the cars. With your neighbour, discuss why people like vintage cars. Present your views to the class.

Photo 1:

Ford Gran Torino, 1972

Photo 2:

Mercedes-Benz 190 SL Coupé, 1962

For the teacher:
Possible reasons for having or desiring a vintage car: nostalgia ("dreaming of better times"); aesthetic reasons; individuality; financial investment ("a beautiful piggy bank")

Pre-viewing Activities II

Worksheet   American Dreams – Overview

Tasks:

1. Do the tasks given to your group and present them. Make use of the pictures and the maps.
2. Add a very short summary of your group's text for the overview grid.
3. Take notes while the other groups present their results.

No.	Short Title	Brief Summary
1	The Korean War	
2	Memories of the Korean War	
3	Vietnam and the Hmong	
4	Vietnamese Boat People	
5	The Law on Refugees	
6	Hmong in America: Mee Moua and Her Family	
7	Hmong in Minnesota	

For the teacher:

The following should be included:

No.	Short Title	Brief Summary
1	The Korean War	In 1950 US military forces step in to help South Korea against an invasion from the communist North, backed by the Soviets. There is a high loss of civilian lives, as well as military. After a stalemate at the 38th parallel, peace negotiations end in a ceasefire in 1953.
2	Memories of the Korean War	Col. Idol will never forget the many displaced people and the plight of the war orphans who begged for food. Two-year-long peace negotiations ended in a ceasefire in 1953. When Col. Idol, who worked as a medic, returned, there was no official military welcome.
3	Vietnam and the Hmong	Hmong people tried to keep their independence, when communist rulers in Laos came into power. They were recruited by the CIA to fight with them in Vietnam. When the war ended, many left, but some stayed. There is still a group living in a hidden rebel camp.
4	Vietnamese Boat People	The term Vietnamese Boat People is also used for those who fled Laos and Cambodia at the end of the Vietnam war because they fought on the side of the US. Many drowned or were prevented from landing. Large numbers settled in the US, Australia, Canada and Europe.
5	The Law on Refugees	Until 1975 there was no program for refugees; they had no claim to enter the US. The law established in 1975 helped those fleeing from the aftermath of the Vietnam War and is still in force.
6	Hmong in America: Mee Moua and her family	Mee Moua's father served with the US forces as a medic in Laos. In 1975, when she was five, they had to flee to escape certain death at the hands of the Pathet Lao. After a stay in a refugee camp in Thailand they came to the US. She is now a Democratic Party activist.
7	Hmong in Minnesota	The Hmong community in Minnesota celebrates 40 years in the US with an exhibition in the Twin Cities to keep Hmong culture alive. They look back to when they came to this mainly white place where they experienced racism. Hmong have built businesses and raised families. The young are more American than Hmong.

Further Suggestion:

In addition to the material suggested for Group 1, one can also use the summary provided on this site (http://www.history.com/this-day-in-history/korean-war-begins) which commemorates the beginning of the Korean War and includes Chinese intervention:

June 25th, 1950 – This Day in History

Korean War begins

It will be easier for students to understand the divided state of the Koreas if one goes back a step and points out that before WW II, Korea was a Japanese possession. When the Allied Forces won the war, Korea was divided into two zones of occupation along the 38th parallel: a Northern, Russian one, and a Southern, American one. As in Germany, the "temporary" division soon became permanent with the Russians assisting the establishment of a Communist regime in the North and the Americans supporting the South financially, militarily and ideologically.

Overview in Pictures, Maps and Photos:

1. In a speech in 1954, President Dwight Eisenhower explains the domino theory.

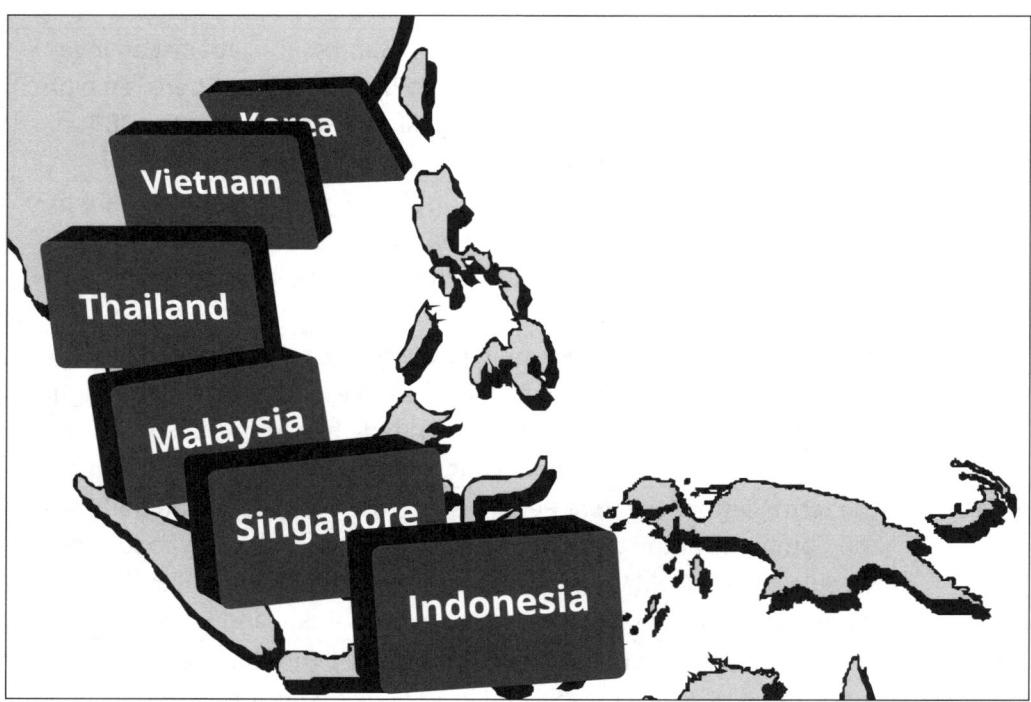

2. A gun crew and their 105-millimetre Howitzer; Korea, July 1950

3. An American soldier interrogates two captured Korean boys who were serving with the North Korean Communist forces

4. Map of the Koreas

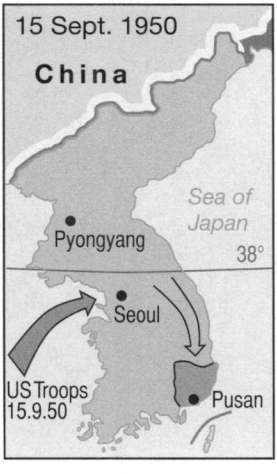
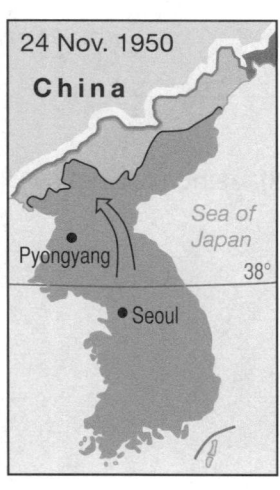

The Korean War 1950 – 1953

South Korea

North Korea

——— line of demarcation
to 25 June 1950 /
38th parallel

——— line of demarcation
from 27 November 1951,
border since ceasefire
of 27 July 1953

0   100   200 km

5. Map of Southeast Asia

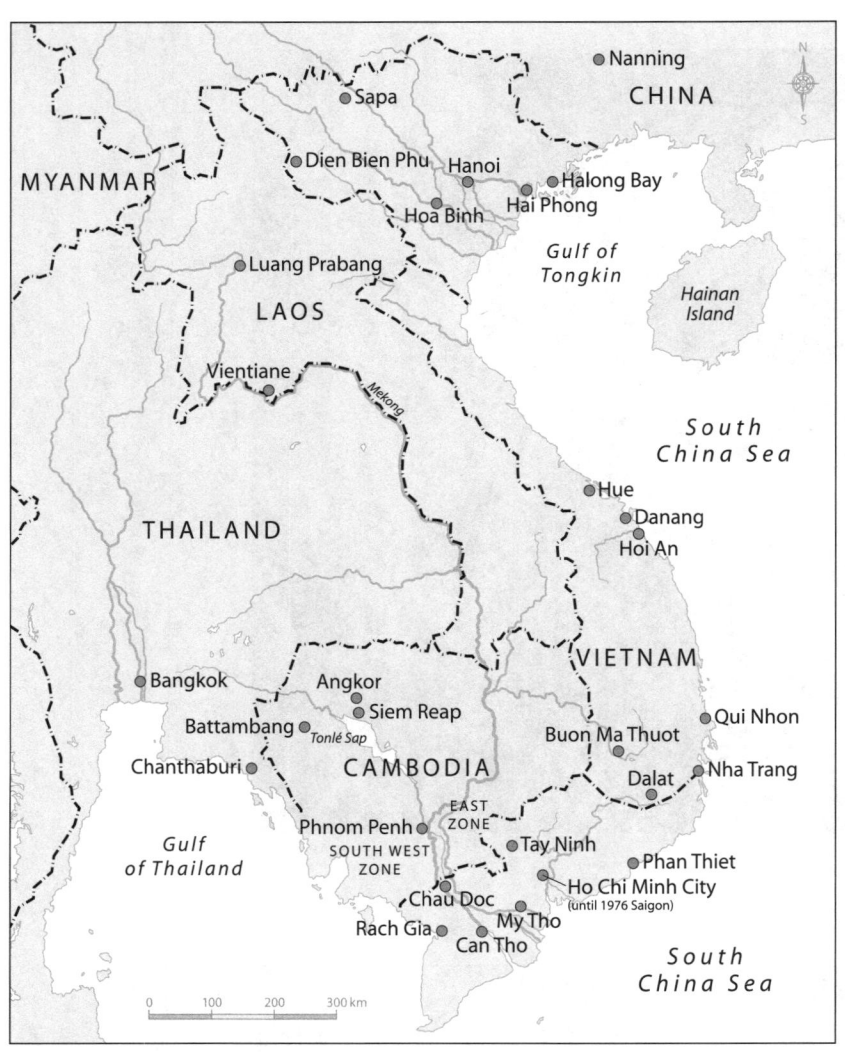

6. Vietnamese Boat People (1978), being rescued by UNHCR

7. In a temporary camp near the border, Cambodian refugees are waiting for medical checks (Klong Kai, Thailand; 1979).

8. The idyllic island of Pulau Bidong, Malaysia, becomes a refugee camp after the fall of Saigon (1975). Several millions of people are left stranded there for years.

Worksheet   American Dream, Group 1: Fighting for America

Tasks:

1. Present the most important facts with the help of a map.
2. Watch the clip from the History Channel and present the **5 Things to Know**.
   https://www.youtube.com/watch?v=h1wFrXKanC0
   Also explain the saying: "Good fences make good neighbours."

The Korean War

The spread of Communism in Korea led to a battle that was brief yet bloody, and a national divide that exists to this day.

On June 25, 1950, the Korean War began when some 75,000 soldiers from the North Korean People's Army poured across the 38th parallel, the boundary between the Soviet-backed Democratic People's Republic of Korea to the north and the pro-Western Republic of Korea to the south. This invasion was the first military action of the Cold War. By July, American troops had entered the war on South Korea's behalf. As far as American officials were concerned, it was a war against the forces of international communism itself. After some early back-and-forth across the 38th parallel, the fighting stalled and casualties mounted with nothing to show for them. Meanwhile, American officials worked anxiously to fashion some sort of armistice with the North Koreans. The alternative, they feared, would be a wider war with Russia and China – or even, as some warned, World War III. Finally, in July 1953, the Korean War came to an end. In all, some 5 million soldiers and civilians lost their lives during the war. The Korean peninsula is still divided today.

The Korean War: 5 Things To Know
https://www.youtube.com/watch?v=h1wFrXKanC0

#1: The 38th parallel

#2: Containment

#3: The Slog of War

#4: Stalemate

#5: Peace?

Worksheet   American Dream, Group 2: Fighting for America

Tasks:

1. Which aspects of the Korean War will stay in this veteran's memory forever?
2. What does he mention about peace?
3. Why does he call it "The Forgotten War"?

Extract: Memories of the Korean War: From Farm Boy to Soldier
Retired Col. Paul E. Idol
www.accesskansas.org/kskoreanwar/stories/story_idol2.html

Other than fighting wars, the average soldier goes through many experiences that are sometimes more memorable, and, at times, more traumatic, than war itself. My war was the Korean War, 1952-53.

[...] From Eta Jima, we went by rail to the seaport of Sasebo for shipment to Korea. We were issued all of our fighting gear at this port. A large sign in the dock area read "Through this port pass the best damn soldiers in the world." I was hoping the sign was right. We crossed the Japanese Sea on flat bottom landing crafts, and we slept on the bottom of the craft in our sleeping bags. What a rough ride it was!

The foggy, rough mountainous coastline of the South Korean peninsula near Pusan will stay in my memory forever. Somewhere in this troubled land, our journey would end, hopefully for only a short period of time. This is the "land of the morning calm," but in 1950-53, the mornings in this small Asian country were anything but calm. This we would see for ourselves in just a few days.

We disembarked from the landing crafts at the Port of Pusan, one of the largest cities on the Southern Coast of the Korean Peninsula. This city had become the sanctuary for hundreds of thousands of South Korean refugees who had fled the North Korean invasion forces early in the war. The city was a mass of hungry, dirty and homeless people living in despair.

We boarded a narrow gauge train that would take us north to the war zone, somewhere near the 38th parallel, approximately 200 miles. We quickly noticed the children of war that congregated along the railroad tracks. Whenever we stopped, we gave them C-rations or whatever food items we had to spare. The kids were orphans, living day-by-day in cardboard or corrugated tin shelters or in caves nearby. Some of the older ones were taking care of their younger brothers or sisters. It was winter and there was not a soldier on the train that was not concerned about the welfare and future of these children. It was too painful to even think about.

As we approached central South Korea, we could see the physical damage caused by the war – remains of railroad engines and cars along the tracks, deserted villages and large bridges hanging in the rivers, destroyed by one side or the other. We were beginning to realize that our destiny was directly ahead of us in Kumhwa Valley.

We had been hearing and reading about the Korean War for several years. We had trained for six months to prepare for it and now we were quickly becoming part of it. [...]

It didn't take long for them to assign me to Baker Company as a medic. This was my home and these men were my family for the next six months, or until the war ended on July 27, 1953. We were in the field all this time during the winter, spring and summer campaigns. There were no permanent wood or brick buildings in the country, except those in the larger cities. The infantry had no opportunity to occupy fixed housing in the rural or mountainous areas. It was always bunkers, pup tents or squad tents. It was a rough life, but we were soldiers and we were young. [...]

Peace negotiations had been going on between the communist forces and the U.N. since 1951, but there always seemed to be items on proposed treaties that they could not agree on. Finally, on July 27, 1953, a treaty was signed and the shooting came to a halt. Everyone was relieved because of the cease-fire, but many were apprehensive about how long it would last.

The ceasefire did work and we continued to train and maintain defensive positions along the 38th parallel. We also assisted in the repatriation of prisoners of war through Peace Village at Panmunjom. We also had time to improve our own conditions and our lives gradually changed for the better. More free time, better food, better quarters (still tents), showers and clean clothes and time to see the countryside. [...]

I made it home, even though I had to ride a WWII Victory ship back across the Pacific. It was a larger and better troop ship than the old Liberty ship that took me to Korea, but it was still one of the terrible experiences of my life. We sailed under the Golden Gate Bridge and the Oakland Bay Bridge before docking in Oakland. We were not greeted by a band, or a large crowd, but we didn't really care, we were home and that was enough.

I left some friends in Korea forever, killed-in-action, missing-in-action, bodies never recovered. "The Forgotten War" will never be forgotten by those who served there, nor by the 54,000 families whose loved ones did not return.

Worksheet   American Dream, Group 3: Fighting for America

Tasks:

1. Use the map of Southeast Asia to show the conflicting parties.
2. Point out when and why the Hmong were recruited.
3. What happened to them after the end of the Vietnam War?

The Hmong

The Vietnam War (also called the Vietnam Conflict and the Second Indochina War) pitted North Vietnam and the Viet Cong, their allies in the South, against the government of South Vietnam and their principal ally, the United States. The war officially began in 1954. The conflict occurred during the height of the cold war and the domino theory was on the mind of every US politician. The United States entered the war under the pretence of stopping the spread of communism throughout Southeast Asia. The political leader of North Vietnam was Ho Chi Minh. Ho Chi Minh started the Viet Minh communist party, who became the leaders of the guerrilla tactic fighting force that would terrorise American troops for the duration of the conflict.

The Hmong are an ethnic group from the highlands of Laos. During the Vietnam War a communist movement called the Pathet Lao began to gain power in Laos. The Hmong people, who valued their independence highly, feared that the communists would not respect their autonomy. In the war between the French colonial rulers of Indochina and the communist rebels, the Hmong had fought on the side of the French. When the communist Pathet Lao movement joined the Laotian government, the CIA decided to recruit the Hmong as guerrilla fighters to keep the Pathet Lao from helping their communist allies in the neighbouring country of Vietnam. The Hmong military leader was a man named Vang Pao, also known as "The General". The U.S. government supplied Vang Pao's Royal Laos Army with training, weapons, food and ammunition and the Hmong waged a guerrilla war against the Pathet Lao as well as any Vietnamese communists operating in Laos (which was officially a neutral country; the CIA kept their involvement secret.)

Hmong forces suffered tremendous losses in their fight against the communists. Before the war there were approximately 300,000 to 400,000 Hmong living in the Laotian highlands, but about 100,000 of them were killed in the fighting. Finally Vang Pao began to recruit children between eight and 13 years old to fill the ranks of his depleted force.

The Vietnam conflict continued for 20 years, with total casualty estimates around 2 million people; nearly half of them Vietnamese, Cambodian, and Laotian civilians. The United States lost just over 58,000 soldiers during the war. US involvement in the war peaked in 1969 as the US had over 500,000 soldiers serving a tour in Southeast Asia. This was also the time of the highest opposition to the war. There were countless protests against the war as a large majority of Americans opposed the now 15-year-long conflict. President Nixon signed a treaty in 1973 to withdraw troops from Vietnam and the war officially ended in 1975 as the North Vietnamese overran Saigon and took control of the South Vietnam government reuniting Vietnam as a sovereign nation.

The consequences of the war were devastating for the Hmong people. Some of the Hmong, including Vang Pao, immigrated to the United States after the war. There are now Hmong immigrant communities in a number of Midwestern cities. Many of the Hmong ended up in refugee camps in Thailand, but a remnant of the Royal Laos Army never gave up the struggle. They were still fighting the Laotian government in 2010 when journalist William Lloyd George visited one of their hidden camps in the jungle and wrote his article about "The Secret Army Still fighting Vietnam War."

"I am CIA. In 1970 Mr Jerry gave me this M79 and told me to shoot enemy," Cher Fer says in a perfect American accent, as he waves a battered grenade-launcher in the air.

"We have lost thousands of troops for America – when the Laos soldiers kill us they feel like they have killed an America soldier. The CIA must come and save us."

The fantasy that America will one day come and liberate them has motivated the veterans and their families to struggle on through for the last 30 years. But despite the Hmong rebels' alliance with the CIA, the American government has made little effort to extract them from the jungle.

Bill Lair, the legendary CIA agent who co-ordinated the operation to build an anti-Communist resistance army out of poorly educated jungle tribespeople, defended the Agency's actions. He said that the US originally hired the Hmong and used Thai recruits to train them because the Hmong "were better than anyone else around, every step they took was up or down so they could move a lot faster than the enemy."

When asked if America should now take steps to save them, he replied: "The CIA owes them nothing. We gave them the choice to leave but they decided to stay, thinking they could go back to how they used to live in the mountains."

In the jungle camp, fear is written on all faces, even those of the children. They know their chances of survival are slim.

As the entire group gathers to say farewell, one old lady grabs the journalist's hand and whispers: "I know the communists are going to kill us all … When they do, make sure you tell the world we were here and what they did to us."

http://www.independent.co.uk/news/world/asia/the-secret-army-still-fighting-vietnam-war-1901755.html

Pre-viewing Activities II

Worksheet American Dream, Group 4: Fleeing to America

Tasks:

1. Explain briefly what the term "Vietnamese Boat People" comprises.
2. How many tried to flee? By which means? Why?
3. How many managed to find refuge? Where?

Vietnamese Boat People

The term "Boat People" not only applies to the refugees who fled Vietnam but also to the people of Cambodia and Laos who did the same, but tend to come under the same umbrella term. "Vietnamese Boat People" is often associated with only those in the former South who fled the new Communist government. However, people in what was North Vietnam who had an ethnic Chinese background fled to Hong Kong at the same time fearing some form of retribution from the government in Hanoi.

Despite the end of the Vietnam War in 1975, tragedy for the people of Vietnam continued into 1978-1979. In late 1978, Indo-China degenerated into wholesale confrontation and war between Vietnam and Kampuchea[1] (Cambodia) and China. In December 1978, Vietnam attacked Kampuchea; in February 1979 Vietnam attacked Chinese forces in the north. These two conflicts resulted in a huge number of refugees.

People in what was South Vietnam feared the rule of their communist masters from what had been North Vietnam. Despite the creation of a united Republic of Vietnam in 1975, many in the South feared retribution once it was found out that they had fought against the North during the actual war. The rule exerted in Ho Chi Minh City (formerly Saigon) was repressive since this was seen as a bastion of "Americanisation". Traditional freedoms were few. It has been estimated that 65,000 Vietnamese were executed after the end of the war, with 1 million being sent to prison and re-education camps where an estimated 165,000 died.

Many took the drastic decision to leave the country – an illegal act under the communist government. As an air flight out of Vietnam was out of the question, many took to makeshift boats in an effort to flee to start a new life elsewhere. Fishing boats were used. While perfectly safe for near-shore fishing, they were not built for the open waters. This coupled with the fact that they were chronically overcrowded made any journey into the open seas highly dangerous.

No one can be sure how many people took the decision to flee nor are there any definitive casualty figures. However, the number who attempted to flee has been put as high as 1.5 million. Estimates for deaths vary from 50,000 to 200,000 (Australian Immigration Ministry). The primary cause of death was drowning though many refugees were attacked by pirates and murdered or sold into slavery and prostitution. Some countries in the region, such as Malaya, turned the boat people away even if they did manage to land. Boats carrying the refugees were deliberately sunk offshore by those in them to stop the authorities towing them back out to sea.

Large numbers of these refugees ended up settling in the United States and Europe. The United States accepted 823,000 refugees; Britain accepted 19,000; France accepted 96,000; Australia and Canada accepted 137,000 each.

---

[1] Kampuchea: the Khmer Rouge-controlled state that controlled Cambodia from 1975 until 1979

Worksheet   American Dream, Group 5: Fleeing to America

Tasks:

1. What are the laws concerning legal entry into a country?
2. Explain how Stephen B. Young got involved in refugee law.
3. Which experiences does he describe from the aftermath of the Vietnam War?

Extract: **The Law on Refugees: Our Door Opens Only When We Choose**
It's what I learned, uncomfortably, when I was involved decades ago in the fate of South-east Asians.
Stephen B. Young, Start Tribune, 9 February 2017

The first relevant fact is the status of a person under international law: No one has a right to move to any foreign county.

Legally entering a country happens only by the grace of its sovereign.

The Universal Declaration of Human Rights says only that people have a right to leave and to return to their country and a right to "seek" asylum from persecution in other countries.

The giving of asylum is within the discretion of those other countries.

Importantly, only people in fear of political persecution can qualify for refugee status. Those seeking to improve their lives by moving to another country are considered to be only economic migrants and are not to receive the privileges given to those in flight from oppression.

My learning the law of refugees happened accidentally in March 1975. As a young Wall Street lawyer, I had taken time from work to go down to Washington, D.C., to provoke a refugee program for South Viet-namese nationalists, those who had relied to their detriment on the United States during the Vietnam War and were then facing imminent communist repression and even imprisonment.

In 1975, no one had any claim to enter the U.S. as a refugee. There was no visa program for refugees. Only the Congress in its arbitrary discretion could authorize the entry into America of a fixed number of refugees in any crisis. The refugees had to give their word – their "parole" – to be good Americans, and then they would be admitted to our territory.

I was sitting in Lionel Rosenblatt's State department office as he spoke with the staff assistant to Sen. Edward Kennedy (a high-ranking member of the Senate Judiciary Committee) on how many Vietnamese Kennedy would allow into the U.S.

Lionel capped the phone's mouthpiece with his right hand, turned to me and said, "Kennedy will only accept 150,000. How many Vietnamese do we need to take?"

I blurted out: "Lionel: One million fled the North in 1954, and now they have kids and grandkids. There are a million soldiers and hundreds of thousands of police, teachers, civil servants, and don't forget their families. I'd say we should try to save a million from communist persecution."

Lionel said: "No way, Kennedy will only allow in the same number as the Cubans whom we paroled in 1965." He went back to the phone, accepting the maximum of 150,000.

This number, however, was better than our offer to the Cambodians. A few years later, I was told that in April 1975 we took out 17 families, leaving all the rest to the Khmer Rouge killing fields.

Some 130,000 Vietnamese nationalist men, women and children fleeing communist persecution, one way or another, came into the custody of Americans, and so were welcomed into the United States.

Other Vietnamese nationalists with similar fears of persecution but who were stuck in Vietnam without a way of reaching any American sanctuary had no legal claim to rescue and resettlement in the U.S. No American court had the power to order their admission into our country.

When the Boat People started to flee Vietnam by sea in 1978 and the Hmong started to swim across the Mekong River to enter Thailand, not one of them had a right to land on Thai soil or anywhere else for that matter. The Thai border guards shot people swimming across the river and pushed small boats back out to sea, where their passengers drowned. All legal, but morally horrific.

So to put in place a law that would permit the Boat People and the Hmong and survivors of Pol Pot's cleansing of politically incorrect people from Cambodia, a citizens commission was formed by the International Rescue Committee under Leo Cherne. I was asked to be a member.

We visited squalid refugee holding sites in Thailand, Malaysia and the Philippines. We lobbied the Carter administration and Sen. Kennedy. With our help, the administration secured a law from Congress on the admission of refugees to replace the vague scope of the parole process. We live by that law today.

Later, Gen. John Vessey of Minnesota, with special authority from President Ronald Reagan, negotiated with Hanoi to release, so that we could give them asylum, political prisoners confined to concentration camps and the children of American soldiers, and their families.

Outside of our federal immigration and naturalization law, no foreign person has any claim on our courts to be admitted to his country.

http://www.startribune.com/the-law-on-refugees-our-door-opens-only-when-we-choose/413352233/

Worksheet   American Dream, Group 6: Settling in America

Tasks:

1. Point out the various stages in Moua's life until her family settled in Minnesota.
2. Which experiences of discrimination did she make and how did she cope?
3. What do we learn about her father and their escape from Laos?

Extract: **Hmong in America: Story of Mee Moua and Her Family**
Jeffrey Hays, http://factsanddetails.com/asian/cat66/sub417/item2742.html

Marc Kaufman wrote in Smithsonian magazine, "Moua's own story embodies the ascendancy of her people." Born in a mountain village in Laos in 1969, she and her family spent three years in a Thai refugee camp before they resettled in Providence, Rhode Island, and from there moved to Appleton, Wisconsin, where her father eventually found work in a television-components factory. After the plant closed, he worked at odd jobs, including a mundane occupation shared by many unskilled, illiterate Hmong newly arrived in the Midwest, "collecting night-crawlers." Moua's family harvested worms in Wisconsin when she was a girl. "It was hard and pretty yucky," she recalls, "but we were always looking for ways to make a little cash." [Source: Marc Kaufman, Smithsonian magazine, September 2004]

"Moua's persistence and capacity for hard work would carry her a long way in a culture whose leaders traditionally have been neither female nor young. She graduated from Brown University in 1992 and went on to earn a law degree from the University of Minnesota in 1997. By her early 30s, Moua had become a prominent Democratic Party activist and a fundraiser for the late U.S. senator Paul Wellstone. In January 2002, Moua won office in a by-election held after a state senator was elected mayor of St. Paul; she was re-elected that fall by a district that is more than 80 percent non-Hmong. Today she travels the nation talking about how the United States finally gave the Hmong a fair shot at opportunity." [Ibid]

Recalling the time local toughs showed up at her house in Appleton, when she was about 12 years old, Moua said, they pelted the house with eggs. She wanted to confront the group, some of whom she suspected had been among those who had earlier defaced the house with racial epithets, but her parents intervened. "Go out there now, and maybe you will get killed, and we won't have a daughter," she remembers her father saying. Her mother added, "Stay inside, work hard and make something with your life: maybe someday that boy will work for you and give you respect." Moua paused. "When I go to places around the country now," she concluded, "I'm very happy to tell you that I get respect."

Moua's father, Chao Tao Moua, was 16 when he was recruited in 1965 by the CIA to work as a medic. For the next ten years, he served with U.S. forces in Laos, setting up remote clinics to treat Hmong villagers and injured American airmen. Then, in 1975, several months after U.S. forces abruptly withdrew from Vietnam in April, victorious Laotian communists (the Pathet Lao) officially seized control of their country. Mee Moua's father and other members of the CIA-backed secret Laotian army knew they were marked men. "One night, some villagers told my father that the Pathet Lao were coming and were looking for whomever worked with the Americans," she says. "He knew he was on their list." Chao Tao Moua, his wife Vang Thao Mous, 5-year-old daughter Mee and infant Mang, later named Mike, fled in the middle of the night from their village in the Xieng Khoung Province. They were among the fortunate who managed to cross the Mekong River into Thailand. Thousands of Hmong died at the hands of the Pathet Lao in the aftermath of the war.

Pre-viewing Activities II

Tasks:

1. Collect facts about the Hmong community in Minnesota.
2. What are the aims of this exhibition?
3. Which personal observations does Wameng Moua add?

Extract: **Hmong Minnesotans memorialized in new exhibit**
Patrick Larkin, LillieNews.com, 9 March 2015

They're here, they're growing, and they're youthful – the average Hmong person in Minnesota is only 19.7 years old, and nearly half of the Hmong in the state are under the age of 18.

They began arriving here 40 years ago, integrating into a very white-centric Twin Cities metro, and steadily finding success and putting down roots.

So, in celebration of 40 years of Hmong people in Minnesota, an exhibit titled "We are Hmong Minnesota" runs March 7 through November 29, 2015 at the Minnesota History Center in St. Paul.

Jessica Kohen, Minnesota History Center marketing director, says part of the motivation for doing the exhibit is that "there's still a lot of confusion about who the Hmong are."

Hmong people first started immigrating to the United States in sizeable numbers in 1975, after the invasion of Laos by North Vietnamese forces during the Vietnam War. Forced out of their homeland, they ended up in refugee camps along the Mekong River in Thailand before moving across the globe.

And they came to Minnesota in large numbers.

The Twin Cities now has one of the largest Hmong populations in the country, and they make up the biggest group of individuals of Asian descent in the state. And as is easy to observe from the vibrant Hmong Village shopping center on Johnson Parkway, and from demographic data, the East Side contains a large population of Hmong people, who've grown families and businesses for decades in the area.

For Noah Vang, co-curator, the exhibit is one way to try to keep Hmong peoples' stories and culture alive. "A lot of our parents who came here are illiterate," he notes, but they have stories to tell.

Those stories of struggle, going through the war and the refugee camps, tell of Hmong perseverance, which Vang states is "what makes this community what it is today."

For Wameng Moua, editor of Hmong Today, the exhibit is in part a tribute to the Hmong elders, many of whom are frail and near the end of their lives. "We wanted to give them something to be proud of," he says. "It's been 40 years since the fall of Saigon, the end of the Vietnam War, and we are American remnants from that war," he points out. The Hmong were recruited by the United States to fight the North Vietnamese.

He adds that without the Americans contacting the Hmong, "we might not have existed in the lexicon of modern thinking . . . we were an obscure people. We were like National Geographic-type people."

In Laos, before and during the war, Hmong people lived an agrarian lifestyle. They traditionally lived in high elevation, often above 3,000 feet. Many families also raised domestic animals, including chicken and pigs.

"A lot of people don't know, but Hmong people . . . we were literally barefooted people, bare-breasted people, just 40 years ago." But now "we have millionaires, politicians, and normal people who just have normal jobs," he says. "We are just as normal as any Minnesotan now."

"Just 40 years ago it's the whitest state in America, and now it's like bustling with diversity," he says.

The East Side has changed a lot since he was a child. He grew up around Case Avenue and Arcade Street, and back in the 1980's, he remembers, "It was very common for us to face blatant racism. Even grown adults would call you 'Chink' and 'Gook.'"

That type of overt racism is luckily not something his kids face, he says, and the East Side has opened up culturally.

Moua adds that his own children lack understanding about what it means to be Hmong. Though he and his wife try to keep Hmong culture alive in their kids, he admits it's a struggle.

They try to teach their youngsters how to speak Hmong, but they're resistant. They're drawn to the television, and end up being more focused on English language and American culture, he says.

"I want them to know the sacrifices and the long journey we took to get here for them to enjoy America."

http://www.bulletin-news.com/articles/2015/03/09/hmong-minnesotans-memorialized-new-exhibit

* * *

Further task:

Go to https://www.mprnews.org/topic/hmong-in-minnesota. (6min 44sec)
"We are Hmong Minnesota": A 40-year journey, remembered, from March 2nd, 2015. Listen to the report by Sasha Aslanian to find out more about the Hmong people who came to Minnesota in 1975 to build new lives.
Present what you consider most important.

Pre-viewing Activities II

Worksheet   Research on the Hmong Ethnic Group

Tasks:

1. Go to http://factsanddetails.com/asian/cat66/sub417/item2744.html
    Under the heading Ethnic Minorities-Hill Tribes find out more about Hmongs.
2. Work in pairs or small groups. Present your answers to the class. Fill in the overview grid.

Group 1: **Population and living areas**	
Group 2: **Languages and writing**	
Group 3: Religion	
Group 4: Spirits	
Group 5: Folk beliefs	
Group 6: Sacrifices	
Group 7: Women and men	
Group 8: Families	

For the teacher:

Group 1: **Population and living areas**	Worldwide, there are an estimated 12 million Hmong, 7.4 million of whom live in China (1990), 300,000 in Vietnam, 200,000 in Laos, 50,000 in Thailand. About a million have resettled in Western countries, including 300,000 in the US.
Group 2: **Languages and writing**	There are five main Hmong-Yao languages sub-divided into dialects. No written language existed until the 1950s. The traditionally oral culture was passed on through the use of story clothes.
Group 3: **Religion**	Hmong beliefs have been influenced by Taoism and Buddhism. Most Hmong are animists who believe that illnesses are caused by spirits and can be healed by shamans. Some Hmong have converted to Christianity.
Group 4: **Spirits**	Hmong believe in a variety of spirits, associated with the house, nature, ancestors. Ceremonies renew the general protection of the household.
Group 5: **Folk beliefs**	Almost every aspect of daily life is affected by folk beliefs. Hmong tie cotton strings around their wrists to ward off evil spirits; they follow old customs in order not to offend the ancestors and to appease the spirits.
Group 6: **Sacrifices**	Animal sacrifices are made at spirit ceremonies, often pigs, also chicken. During big ceremonies a cow is offered. While the spirits take the soul of the sacrifice, the meat is consumed by the household/village.
Group 7: **Women and men**	There are strict gender roles. Women are responsible for all household chores and child care, plus regular farming tasks. Men fell trees and hunt. Planting, harvesting and threshing, for example, are shared tasks.
Group 8: **Families**	Traditionally, households consist of extended families; today there are also nuclear families. Children help with chores and learn subsistence skills.

U.S. Immigration Timeline

20,000 years ago	Most scientists believe that human beings first came to America over the Bering Straits about 20,000 years ago. They are the ancestors of many Native American cultures.
~ 1000	A small number of Vikings arrive.
1492	Columbus reaches the Americas (= North America, South America, Caribbean); he is followed by other European explorers.
1502	Africans are brought as slaves to the island of Hispanola (present-day Dominican Republic and Haiti) by the Spanish, with over 10 million enslaved Africans yet to arrive on the shores of the Americas.
1607	The first permanent English colony is built in Jamestown, Virginia.
1619	The first Africans (a group of around twenty) arrive at Jamestown, Virginia as indentured servants. By 1680, there are about 7,000 African slaves in the American colonies, and by 1790 around 700,000, according to some estimates.
1620	A group of roughly 100 people later known as the Pilgrims flee religious persecution in Europe and arrive at present-day Plymouth, Massachusetts where they establish a colony. They are soon followed by a larger group seeking religious freedom, the Puritans, who establish the Massachusetts Bay Colony. An estimated 20,000 Puritans migrate to the region between 1630 and 1640.
1700-1776	**First large immigrant wave: Europeans, mostly English, arrive in massive numbers**, seeking economic opportunities. Many come as indentured servants since the passage is expensive. Additionally, thousands of English convicts are shipped across the Atlantic as indentured servants.
1750	Population reaches more than one million.
1790	Population reaches almost four million, of which the English are the largest ethnic group. Nearly 20% are of African descent. Significant numbers of German, Scottish and Irish residents are registered; Native Americans are not counted in this first Census. The **1790 Naturalization Act** establishes the country's first uniform rule for naturalisation. The law provides that "free white persons" who have resided in the United States for at least two years may be granted citizenship, so long as they demonstrate good moral character and swear allegiance to the Constitution. Children (under 21) of naturalised citizens also become US citizens.
1800s	Immigration is light, around 6,000 people a year on average, including French refugees from the revolt in Haiti (1796-1804). America is becoming "the asylum for the persecuted lovers of civil and religious liberty from every part of Europe." (Thomas Paine)
1808	Congress makes it illegal to bring slaves to the United States, but the practice continues.
1820-1870	**Second large immigrant wave: About 7.5 million arrive, mainly from northern and western Europe (especially Great Britain, Ireland, and western Germany)**, fuelled by the beginning Industrial Revolution, the end of the slave trade and the westward movement. About 5 million immigrants from Germany settle in the US in the 19th century. In the national census of 2000, more than 40 million Americans claim German ancestry – more than any other group except the British.
1840s	A wave of Irish immigrants arrives, escaping famine because of potato crop failure. In the 1840s, almost half of America's immigrants are from Ireland alone. All in all, around 1.5 million Irish people die during the Great Hunger; about as many flee to America.
1848	The discovery of gold lures around 25,000 Chinese and large numbers of Latin American immigrants to the west coast.

1864	The Republican platform of 1864 states "Foreign immigration which in the past has added so much to the wealth, resources and increase of power to the nation [...] should be fostered and encouraged." The **Immigration Act of 1864** establishes the position of the Commissioner of Immigration, who will report to the Secretary of State, and provides that labour contracts made by immigrants outside the United States shall be enforceable by US courts. It legalises the importation of contract labour.
1861-1865	The US Civil War results in the emancipation of approximately 4 million slaves. The Emancipation Declaration of 1863 also permits African-American men to enlist in the Union army.
1870s	Following the Civil War, the US experiences a depression which contributes to a slowdown in immigration.
1881-1920	**Third large immigrant wave: Nearly 23.5 million arrive, mainly from southern and eastern Europe (especially Austro-Hungary, Italy, and Russia)**, during times of rapid industrialisation and urbanisation.
1882	The **Immigration Act of 1882** is one of the first attempts to broad federal oversight of immigration. Taxes are levied for each (non-US citizen) passenger arriving from a ship from a foreign port to be paid by the ship's owner and to proceed into the Treasury's "immigration fund". The law further establishes the screening of arriving passengers: anyone deemed a "convict, lunatic, idiot, or person unable to take care of himself or herself without becoming a public charge" shall not be allowed to land.
1882	The first **Chinese Exclusion Act** is passed. For the first time, immigration is regulated along racial lines. It suspends the immigration of Chinese labourers for ten years, but allows those Chinese who were in the US as of November 17, 1880 to remain. However, resident Chinese are denied U.S. citizenship.
1886	The Statue of Liberty is unveiled. Though not initially sculpted and erected as a symbol of immigration, it quickly becomes so as immigrant ships pass under the torch and shining face headed towards Ellis Island: it offers "world-wide welcome" to the "tired", the "poor" and the "huddled masses", as Emma Lazarus phrases it.
1888	The **1888 Scott Act** further restricts Chinese immigration by prohibiting lawfully residing Chinese nationals who departed the United States from returning, even when such nationals previously received certificates authorising their re-admission.
1892	**Act to Prohibit the Coming of Chinese Persons into the United States**; known as the Geary Act. The law extends the prohibitions of the 1882 Chinese Exclusion Act for an additional ten years and requires all Chinese nationals residing in the United States to obtain certificates indicating their lawful presence.
1892	Ellis Island opens. Teenager Annie Moore from County Cork, Ireland, is the first immigrant processed at Ellis Island. She made the nearly two-week journey across the Atlantic Ocean in steerage with her two younger brothers. More than 12 million immigrants will enter the US through Ellis Island during its years of operation from 1892 to 1954.
1900	Population reaches 76 million.
1907	A record total of 1.3 million enter the country legally in this year, of which one million pass through Ellis Island.
1910	Angel Island Immigration Center, located in San Francisco Bay, operates from 1910 until 1940 when it is destroyed in a fire (and with it, all records). While Ellis Island processes European immigrants, people from China, Japan, Russia and South Asia (in that order) are detained and interrogated in Angel Island – and often sent back. It is one of the 24 ports of entry established by the U.S. government to process and detain immigrants entering and leaving.

1914	World War I inspires strong anti-immigration feelings. Immigration figures decline.
1917	The **1917 Immigration Act** creates an "Asiatic barred zone" covering British India, most of Southeast Asia, and almost all of the Middle East. Nationals from countries within the zone are prohibited from immigrating, though the law exempts students, as well as certain professionals (e.g., teachers, government officers, lawyers, physicians, and chemists) and their wives and children. Immigrants over 16 years old are required to pass literacy tests.
1921	The **1921 Emergency Quota Act** limits the number of immigrants of each nationality allowed to immigrate to the US each year to 3 percent of the number of foreign-born persons of that nationality present in the United States as of the 1910 census. Temporary visitors, government officials and nationals of Western hemisphere countries are excluded from the quotas.
1924	The **1924 National Origins Quota Act** (known as the Johnson-Reed Act) establishes that quotas will be calculated based on 2 percent of each nationality's proportion of the foreign-born US population in 1890, as indicated in the 1890 census. This is criticised as discriminating against southern and eastern Europeans who arrived in large numbers after that date. Students, nationals of Western Hemisphere countries, members of certain professions, and the wives and minor children of US citizens are exempt from the quotas.
1930-1965	**Immigration declines** due to restrictive laws, the Great Depression, World War II and the Cold War. Between 1930 and 1950, America's foreign-born population decreases from 14.2 to 10.3 million, or from 11.6 to 6.9 percent of the total population.
1930s	A small number of refugees fleeing Nazi persecution arrive under the quota system, but most are turned away.
1942	After the declaration of war against the Axis Powers, German and Italian resident aliens are detained. But for the Japanese, the policies are more extreme: President Franklin D. Roosevelt's Executive Order No. 9066 strips both resident aliens and American-born citizens of Japanese descent of their civil liberties. Persons of Japanese ancestry are interned in ten "relocation centers" without due process or hard evidence. They are considered "security risks" even though young Japanese Americans are volunteering for military service. Justice Murphy is one of the three dissenting voices when the Supreme Court upholds the decision in 1944. He says that "the broad provisions of the Bill of Rights" are not "suspended by the mere existence of a state of war. Distinctions based on color and ancestry are utterly inconsistent with our traditions and ideals." Not until 1988 does Congress officially apologise for the internment of 110,000 to 120,000 Japanese-Americans, many of whom lost their businesses, farms and real estate during their imprisonment.
1942	The **1942 Bracero Agreement** allows Mexican nationals to enter the United States to serve as temporary agricultural workers. They are needed to supplement the depleted workforce. The agreement is extended in 1949 and 1951 and continues in some form until 1964. More than 5 million Mexicans come and hundreds of thousands stay. Ironically, at the same time, after the war, another government programme begins a campaign of deportations which lasts well into the 1950s. More than 4 million immigrants, as well as many Mexican Americans, are sent to Mexico.
1942	The **Magnuson Act** repeals the Chinese Exclusion Acts and allows Chinese nationals to become US citizens and to become eligible to vote.
1945	Puerto Ricans begin to arrive in large numbers.
1945	The **War Brides Act** authorises the admission of the foreign-born spouses and children of US citizens serving in or honourably discharged from the armed forces during World War II.

1947	The refugee crisis after the war makes President Truman appeal to Congress: "I urge the Congress to turn its attention to this world problem in an effort to find ways whereby we can fulfill our responsibilities to these thousands of homeless and suffering refugees of all faiths."
1948	The **Displaced Persons Act of 1948** allows over 200,000 individuals displaced from their homelands by Nazi persecution to immigrate to the United States. Millions, however, are left to seek refuge elsewhere.
1952	The **Immigration and Nationality Act** (known as the McCarren-Walter Act) preserves the national-origins quota system in an updated version. For the first time, Asian nations are assigned quotas that allow their nationals to immigrate to the US. The law also establishes that US consular officers will screen foreign nationals for admissibility to the United States, and that officers will not issue visas to individuals found inadmissible. Japanese Americans and other Asian Americans can now become U.S. citizens and vote; this right has been granted to Asian Indians in 1946 already.
1953	The **Refugee Relief Act of 1953** authorises the admission of up to 205,000 non-quota immigrants who are fleeing persecution or have been expelled from their homes in Europe.
1954	Ellis Island closes, marking an end to mass immigration.
1956	38,000 Hungarians who flee from a failed uprising against the Soviets are among the first Cold War refugees admitted to the US between 1956 and 1957.
1962	The **Migration and Refugee Assistance Act of 1962** authorises funds to assist foreign nationals from the Western Hemisphere who have fled their countries of origin because of persecution or fear of persecution on account of race, religion, or political opinion. It assists Cuban nationals fleeing Communism after the communist revolution in Cuba in 1959.
1965	The **1965 Immigration and Nationality Act** (known as the Hart-Cellar Act) abolishes the national-origins quota system and replaces it with a system in which immigrants are admitted based on their relationship to a US citizen or lawful permanent resident family member or US employer. This effectively ends a system that favours white Europeans over other races. Caps are placed on the total number of immigrants admitted each year (exempting "immediate relatives" – spouses, parents and minor children – of US citizens). Beginning in 1968, a cap of 120,000 is introduced for immigrants from the Western Hemisphere countries.
1965	Immigration from Asia and the West Indies increases; within five years Asian immigration quadruples.
1975	The **1975 Indochina Migration and Refugee Assistance Act** expands the definition of the term "refugee", as defined in the Migration and Refugee Assistance Act of 1962, to include individuals fleeing persecution or fear of persecution from Cambodia and Vietnam.
1976	The **Immigration and Nationality Act Amendments of 1976** adopts the 1965 Immigration and Nationality Act's system of immigration "preference categories" (family ties; special job skills, e.g. doctors, nurses, scientists, specialists) for immigrants from Western Hemisphere countries.
1980	The **Refugee Act of 1980** establishes a new system for processing and admitting refugees from overseas as well as asylum seekers physically present at US borders or in the country.
1986	The government gives amnesty to nearly 3 million aliens through the **Immigration Reform and Control Act (IRCA)**, which also imposes sanctions on employers who knowingly hire or recruit unauthorised immigrants. The law creates two legalisation programmes. One allows unauthorised aliens who have lived in the United States since 1982 to regularise their status; the other permits people who have worked for at least 90 days in certain agricultural jobs to apply for permanent resident status. Roughly 2.7 million people thus eventually become lawful permanent residents.

1988	The **Anti-Drug Abuse Act** adds "aggravated felony" as a new ground for deportation. Initially, this category is limited to serious crimes (e.g., murder and drug and weapons trafficking), regardless of the sentence imposed and the longevity of the alien's residence in the United States.
1989	Sen. Edward Kennedy introduces the Diversity Visa Lottery, which allows 50,000 permanent resident visas (green cards) per year, selected from countries of low immigration rates over the previous five years. Requirements include high school education, at least 2 years of work experience, and no criminal background. After intensive vetting by the US Department of State, people are allowed to apply for the lottery.
1990	The **1990 Immigration Act** raises legal admissions to 50 percent above the pre-IRCA level (mainly in the category of employment-based immigrants), eases controls on temporary workers, and limits the government's power to deport immigrants for ideological reasons.
1994	The **Violent Crime Control and Law Enforcement Act** gives the US Attorney General the option to bypass deportation proceedings for alien aggravated felony and enhances penalties for alien smuggling and re-entry after deportation.
1996	The **Antiterrorism and Effective Death Penalty Act** adds new crimes to the definition of aggravated felony.
1996	The **Illegal Immigration Reform and Immigrant Responsibility Act** adds new grounds of inadmissibility and deportability. It also increases the number of Border patrol agents, introduces new border control measures, reduces government benefits available to immigrants, toughens procedures for asylum seekers and other immigrants and mandates an entry-exit system to monitor both arrivals and departures of immigrants.
1997	The **Nicaraguan Adjustment and Central American Relief Act** provides several ways of relief from deportation and adjustment of status for qualified Nicaraguans, Cubans, Salvadorans, Guatemalans, and nationals of former Soviet-bloc countries.
1998	The **Haitian Refugee Immigration Fairness Act** provides similar benefits to qualified Haitian nationals as did NACARA.
2001	After the terrorist attack on the Twin Towers, the **USA Patriot Act** broadens the terrorism grounds for excluding aliens from entering the United States and increases monitoring of foreign students.
2002	The US-VISIT programme is established to implement the **Enhanced Border Security and Visa Entry Reform Act**.
2002	The **Homeland Security Act** creates the Department of Homeland Security which includes, after restructuring, these agencies: US Customs and Border Protection, US Immigration and Customs Enforcement, and US Citizenship and Immigration Services.
2005	The **REAL ID Act** establishes guidelines for removal cases, expands the terrorism-related grounds for inadmissibility and deportation, includes measures to improve border infrastructure, and requires states to verify an applicant's legal status before issuing a driver's license or personal identification card that may be accepted for any federal purpose.
2006	The **Secure Fence Act** mandates the construction of more than 700 miles of double-reinforced fence to be built along the border with Mexico, through the US states of California, Arizona, New Mexico, and Texas in areas that experience illegal drug trafficking and illegal immigration.
2012	The Obama administration launches the **Deferred Action for Childhood Arrivals (DACA) initiative** to provide a temporary reprieve from deportation to qualified unauthorised immigrants who came to the US as children. There are 700,000 beneficiaries of this programme. During the permit's validity (two years; renewable) they will not be deported and can seek employment.

2017	In January, President Donald Trump signs Executive Order 13769 banning refugees and people from seven Muslim-majority countries (Iran, Iraq, Libya, Somalia, Sudan, Syria, and Yemen) from entering the United States. People protesting perceive what is happening as contrary to U.S. tradition since 1965 when immigration laws ended overt discrimination; the President's order clearly favours Christian refugees. The Trump administration announces the termination of the DACA programme within a year, although up to 85% of Americans want the "Dreamers" to remain.
2018	In January, while discussing with lawmakers under which conditions Temporary Protected Status for immigrants from Haiti and Africa might be renewed, President Trump states that he does not want immigrants from "shithole countries" (which he has since unpersuasively denied). He'd prefer immigrants from Norway. Might he be referring to the fact that in the 1880s alone, 9% of the total population of Norway emigrated to America?

Task 1:

Discuss and give answers to the following questions:
1. Does America have a duty to keep its doors open to the world?
2. Can immigrants keep their own culture and language, and still be called Americans?
3. Is continued economic growth in America dependent upon a liberal immigration policy?

Task 2:

Discuss:
"Immigrants bring with them their own histories, traditions and ideas, all of which broaden and enrich our sense of what it means to be an American."

Worksheet   Immigration Patterns

Tasks:

Compare the immigration patterns in these two graphs.

1. 1930-1965

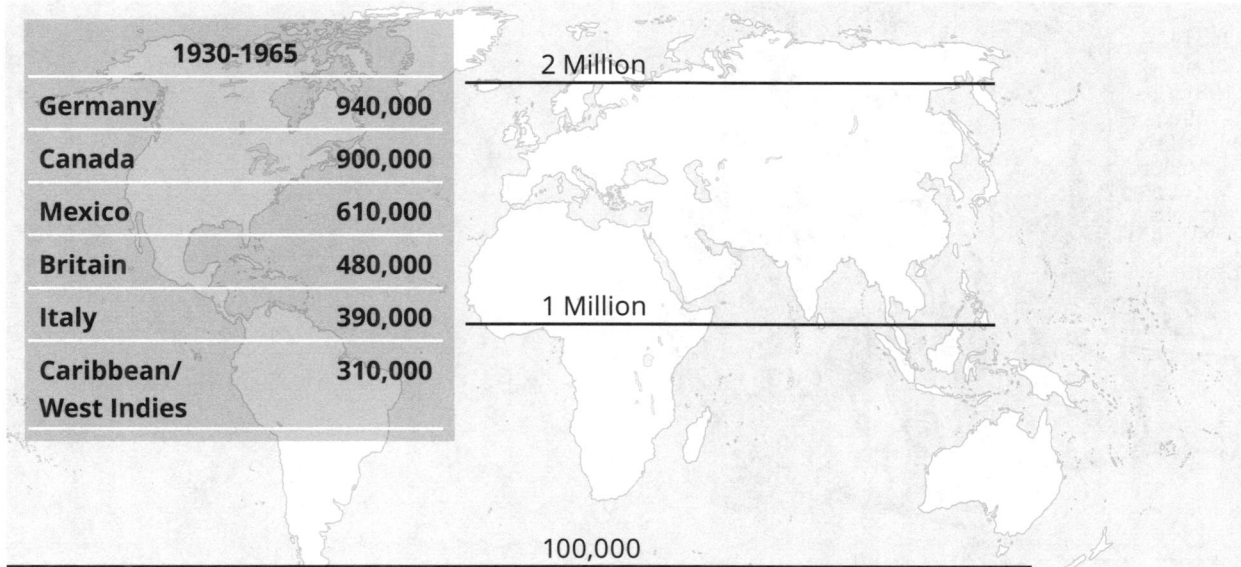

1930-1965	
Germany	940,000
Canada	900,000
Mexico	610,000
Britain	480,000
Italy	390,000
Caribbean/ West Indies	310,000

2 Million

1 Million

100,000

2. 1965-2000

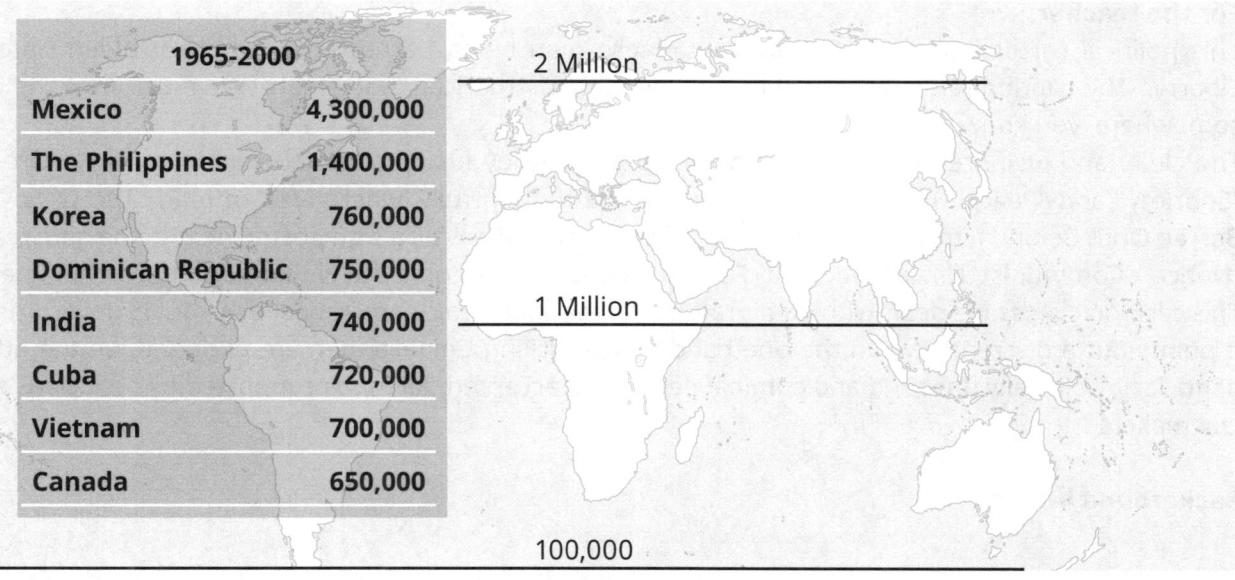

1965-2000	
Mexico	4,300,000
The Philippines	1,400,000
Korea	760,000
Dominican Republic	750,000
India	740,000
Cuba	720,000
Vietnam	700,000
Canada	650,000

2 Million

1 Million

100,000

For the teacher:

There is a clear shift in immigration patterns after the 1965 law. Today the majority of immigrants come from Asia and Latin America rather than Europe.
More information and statistics can be found at https://www.libertyellisfoundation.org/immigration-timeline

Pre-viewing Activities III

Worksheet   Chinese Immigration: "The Only One Barred Out"

Tasks:

Describe, analyse and evaluate this cartoon from 1882.

THE ONLY ONE BARRED OUT.
ENLIGHTENED AMERICAN STATESMAN.—" We must draw the line *somewhere*, you know."

Source: Frank Leslie's illustrated newspaper, vol. 54 (1882 April 1), p. 96

For the teacher:

This political cartoon from 1882 shows a Chinese man being barred entry to the "Golden Gate of Liberty." The caption reads, as if said by an Enlightened American Statesman, "We must draw the line somewhere, you know."

The clean and well-dressed Chinese man is surrounded by his luggage labelled "Industry", "Order", "Sobriety" and "Peace". He is looking to the ground thoughtfully, where we can read "The Only One Barred Out". Behind him, the American flag is flying above the wall; a sign posted next to the gate reads "Notice – Communist, Nihilist, Socialist, Fenian & Hoodlum Welcome But No Admittance to Chinamen."

This cartoon's message deals with immigration and the limits which are imposed by the US government. It points out a discrepancy. On the one hand, hard-working Chinese men are excluded, on the other hand, lazy, politically unsound and criminal people are accepted. All this is supported by politicians and law-makers.

Background info:

- The Chinese Exclusion Act of 1882, which severely restricted immigration from China, was brought about by lawmakers from the West Coast. Although Chinese people composed only .002 percent of the nation's population, Congress passed the act to placate worker demands and to assuage concerns about maintaining white "racial purity".
- Under Jim Crow Laws, Chinese people and people with Chinese ancestors were not allowed to vote.
- The greatest mass lynching in American history happened in Los Angeles in 1871, in which 17 Chinese immigrants were murdered by a mob of around 500 white men.

Pre-viewing Activities III

Worksheet   Refugee Arrivals

Tasks:

Describe the development of refugee arrivals to the US from Southeast Asia. Relate them to political events and decisions.

Refugee Arrivals to the U.S. from Southeast Asia Fiscal Years 1975-2010[3]				
Fiscal Year	Cambodia	Laos	Vietnam	Total
1975	4,600	800	125,000	130,400
1976	1,100	10,200	3,200	14,500
1977	300	400	1,900	2,600
1978	1,300	8,000	11,100	20,400
1979	6,000	30,200	44,500	80,700
1980	16,000	55,500	95,200	166,700
1981	38,194	19,777	65,279	123,250
1982	6,246	3,616	27,396	37,258
1983	13,041	2,907	22,819	38,767
1984	19,727	7,218	24,856	51,801
1985	19,175	5,195	25,222	49,592
1986	9,845	12,313	21,700	43,858
1987	1,786	13,394	19,656	34,836
1988	2,897	14,597	17,571	35,065
1989	2,162	12,560	21,924	36,646
1990	2,329	8,715	27,797	38,841
1991	179	9,232	28,396	37,807
1992	163	7,285	26,795	34,243
1993	63	6,944	31,401	38,408
1994	15	6,211	34,110	40,336
1995	6	3,682	32,250	35,938
1996	5	2,203	16,107	18,315
1997	9	915	6,612	7,536
1998	7	9	10,266	10,282
1999	0	19	9,622	9,641
2000	0	64	2,839	2,903
2001	23	22	3,109	3,154
2002	0	18	2,855	2,873
2003	4	13	1,654	1,371
2004	7	6,005	979	6,991
2005	3	8,517	2,009	10,529
2006	3	830	3,039	3,872
2007	9	117	1,500	1,626
2008	15	59	1,112	1,186
2009	8	14	1,486	1,508
2010	9	36	873	918
Totals	145,230	257,587	771,834	1,174,651

3 Sources: (1) Office of Refugee Resettlement. 1982-2001. Annual Reports to Congress (Fiscal Years 1981-2000). Washington, DC: Office of Refugee Resettlement, Administration for Children and Families, U.S. Department of Health and Human Services. (2) FY 2000-2010 are from the 2010 Yearbook Immigration Statistics, Office of Immigration Statistics, U.S. Department of Homeland Security. (3) Refugee Arrival statistics for FY 1975-1980 are from Rumbaut (2000: 182).

How to Deal with the Film *Gran Torino*

Gran Torino, when it came out in 2008 and though it has an "over 13" recommendation because of strong language and violence, met with enthusiastic reviews. For despite the many racial slurs, the film has a decidedly anti-racist message.

Although *Gran Torino* was considered by the American Film Institute as one of the Ten Best Films of 2008, it was not nominated in any of the 81st Academy Awards categories. Clint Eastwood, who directed the film and convincingly portrayed grumpy Walt Kowalski, won an award for Best Actor from the National Board of Review; the song "Gran Torino" was nominated for the Golden Globe Awards for Best Original Song.

When dealing with the film in class, the students will realise that *Gran Torino* addresses issues of racism, life and death, the meaning of family, guilt and redemption within the context of the relationship of neighbours in suburban Detroit. They will see the bigger issues of ethnic relations, immigration, economic changes in America, life in urban America, violence and conflict resolution.

Various ways of presenting the film are possible.

One might want to start with the trailer and ask the students what they expect from a film that is introduced in this way. The trailer can also be used after viewing the film. Students compare the film and the trailer and point out what has been emphasised in the trailer and what has been left out. For example, when discussing the equivocal statement *"They don't have a chance"* ways of relating it to different characters will turn up.

The following teaching suggestions divide the viewing into six parts. Accompanied by questions and homework tasks the students will explore identity, relationships and belonging with the main characters.

These six parts are suggested; the numbers in brackets indicate the DVD chapters:

Part I:	Neighbours: Walt and the Hmong/Getting to Know Thao (Chapters 1 – 4)
Part II:	Life and Death (Chapters 5 – 10)
Part III:	Parties and Families (Chapters 11 – 13)
Part IV:	Belonging I – Walt and Thao (Chapters 14 – 19)
Part V:	Belonging II – The Gang (Chapters 20 – 23)
Part VI:	Life and Death and the Future (Chapters 24 – 29)

There is an overview grid in which to fill in brief summaries per chapter (pages 35–36); there are tasks which look more closely at the characters and their development (pages 64–66), there are also tasks which look more closely at the role and symbolic meaning of items like the Silver Star Medal and the Gran Torino. For all these tasks, suggested answers are added. The filled-in Chapter overview grid can be found on pages 37 to 43.

Screenshots should be used to talk about relationships, and plot and character development. How to make them and how to deal with them in class can be found on page 75, more on filming, cinematographic terms and some creative ideas on pages 71 to 74.

While-viewing Activities – Gran Torino

Tasks:

While viewing, fill in the chapter by chapter overview. Also state the topics mentioned/dealt with.

Ch.	Where/ When	Who	DVD Chapter Title / What
1			Inevitable Disappointment
2			I confess
3			Men of Their Houses
4			Chill With Us
5			More About Death
6			Attempted Theft
7			Get Off My Lawn
8			We're not in Korea
9			Crazy Old Man
10			That Brother of Yours
11			Unhappy Birthday
12			Not at Peace
13			Fixer and Toad

14			Making Amends
15			Home Improvements
16			Nice Talking to You
17			Helpful Hands
18			Manning Thao Up
19			Construction Job
20			Making Him Look Bad
21			Getting Ugly
22			Targets
23			Pissed-Off Padre
24			What Needs to Be Done
25			At Peace
26			I Finish Things
27			I've Got a Light
28			Last Rites and Wishes
29			End Credits

For the teacher:

The filled-in overview should contain the following:

Ch.	Where/ When	Who	DVD Chapter Title / What
Part I: Neighbours: Walt and the Hmong/Getting to know Thao			
1	At church	Walt Kowalski, his two sons, their wives and children; other mourners; Father Janovich	**Inevitable Disappointment** During the funeral service for his wife Dorothy, Walt is apart from his family. His grandchildren behave disrespectfully: Ashley is wearing a crop top and starts texting during the service; Josh crosses himself murmuring *"Spectacles, testicles, wallet and watch"*. Walt's sons mention that whatever one does will disappoint Walt. When the very young priest starts his sermon saying *"Death is often a bittersweet occasion to us Catholics"*, Walt growls. **loneliness / isolation / family relations / (dis)respect / religion**
2	at Walt's home	Walt Kowalski, his two sons, their wives and children; other mourners; Father Janovich, Thao, dog Daisy	**I Confess** Many mourners come to the funeral reception at Walt's house. He, however, goes to his porch with his dog Daisy. When Walt sees many Asian-looking people enter the house next door, he wonders aloud about *"How many swamp rats can you get in one room"* and spits on the ground; and when Thao from the neighbouring house asks for a favour, Walt sends him away with a racial slur. Father Janovich speaks to him about Dorothy's wish that Walt go to confession. Walt rebukes him. The members of Walt's family want to leave as soon as possible and do not care about him; his grandsons rifle through his belongings and find a war medal; his granddaughter even asks what he plans to do with his vintage car once he dies. He does not need to say anything when his son Mitch and his family leave in their Toyota Land Cruiser: they know that Walt hates their not buying American. **family relations / racism / (dis)respect / religion**
3	next door; same day	The Lors, a Hmong family: Sue, Thao, mother, grandmother, guests; shaman	**Men of Their Houses** The grandmother is dissatisfied with Thao: she wants a man in the house, not someone like Thao who is in the kitchen washing the dishes and *"doing everything his sister says"*. While the shaman is conducting a traditional Hmong baptism ceremony, Thao leaves the house. **gender roles / tradition / family / spirituality**
	in front of and in Walt's home; weeks later	Walt; Hmong grandmother Father Janovich	Walt complains about the deterioration of his neighbourhood; in Hmong, the Hmong grandmother complains about Walt strutting around and not leaving. They both spit to the ground – she wins. The priest comes and tells Walt that he promised Dorothy to look after him and to make sure he goes to confession. Walt openly and disdainfully shows him that he is not interested in religion and that he distrusts the young priest whom he considers *"an over-educated 27-year-old virgin"* *"straight from the seminary"*. **racism / neighbourhood / parallel structures / disrespect**

| 4 | on his way home | Thao, Latino gang, Hmong gang | **Chill with Us**
Thao is on his way home, reading a book, when Latino gang members drive by slowly in their car. Even though they insult him, Thao does not react but walks on reading. His cousin "Spider" (Fong) spots him; he and the Hmong gang come to Thao's rescue and defend their turf. They cannot force Thao to get into their car, but "Smokie", the gang leader, tells him they are going to come for him the next day, which they do. Sue ridicules them and goes inside. The young men keep exerting pressure on Thao until he asks what he has to do. He is to steal his neighbour's car.
gangs / ethnicity / belonging / asserting one's power / peer pressure |
| | next day | Sue, Thao, "Spider", "Smokie" and 3 more gang members | |

Part II: Life and Death

5	in a bar; in the evening	Walt and friends (war veterans); Father Janovich	**More About Death** They are telling racist jokes when Father Janovich comes in. Admiringly, Walt acknowledges the priest's persistence. In a booth, they talk about life and death. Walt recalls bitter war experiences and points out that Father Janovich is too young to know what he is talking about. The priest, however, makes Walt reflect and realise that he may know a lot about death but not much about living. **friendship / religion / faith / trauma of war**
6	in Walt's garage, same night	Walt, Thao	**Attempted Theft** When Walt hears a noise and sees a light in his garage, he loads his M1 Garand and walks in (Note the underlying drum roll!). Aiming the gun at the retreating Thao at close range, Walt stumbles and his shot hits a sign on the wall. Thao runs away. He does not get into the gang's waiting car. Meanwhile, on the garage floor, Walt coughs up blood.
	next day	Mitch	When his son Mitch calls the next day (seemingly to find out how Walt is doing; in reality he wants to get tickets for a Lions match), Walt does not mention any health issues. Walt polishes his Gran Torino and leaves it temptingly in his driveway. **gang initiation / defending one's home and property=standing one's ground / family relations / pride + disdain**
7	in front of the houses; same night	Hmong gang members, Thao, Lor women, Walt	**Get Off My Lawn** The Hmong gang arrive and tell the reluctant Thao that they will give him another chance. They then forcefully drag him to their car while the Hmong women try to stop them. In their scuffle, they break a garden gnome and run onto Walt's lawn. With his assault rifle aimed at them he tells them to get off his lawn (again, underlying drum roll). His intrepid attitude and statements like *I blow a hole in your face ... and sleep like a baby* make them retreat. When Sue thanks him, he orders the women and Thao to get off his lawn, too.
	next morning	Walt, Hmong, Sue, Thao	Walt finds food dishes and flowers from Hmong people in his street on his stairs to thank him for his intervention. He does not accept them and puts them in his bin. Since he does not want any contact with his neighbours, he does not accept Sue's plants or Thao's excuse. Walt does not want to be the hero of the neighbourhood. **gang pressure / violence / defending one's home and property / gratitude / scorn-disdain-cold-heartedness-indifference or fear of commitment?**

8	at Walt's house; same day in the afternoon	Walt, Father Janovich	**We're not in Korea** The priest is angry with Walt for not having called the police because somebody could have been killed. He then resumes their conversation about life and death and begs Walt to go to confession. Convincingly, the priest talks about forgiveness for the terrible acts soldiers are forced to do. But Walt counters saying *"The thing that haunts a man the most is what he isn't ordered to do."* **rule of law / offering peace and forgiveness / trauma of war**
	at the barber shop	Walt, Martin	At the barber shop Walt exchanges friendly banter with Martin, the barber (Dago, Polack, etc.) **language as a means of identification**
9	in the street same day	Sue and her white date Trey, three black gang members, Walt	**Crazy Old Man** Despite being with her white date, Sue is insulted by black gang members. When Trey uses black language and greetings they get aggressive. Sue defends herself verbally and physically – her boyfriend remains passive. Walt, who has been watching from across the street, stops his truck in front of them. He is not intimidated by their threats and imitates pulling out a pistol and pointing at them. He then draws his semi-automatic and orders Sue to get into his truck. **language as a means of identification ("bro"); belonging / threat / reluctant respect** (*Take care now. – You, too.*)
10	in Walt's truck, same day	Walt, Sue	**That Brother of Yours** Walt lectures Sue about her dangerous behaviour. She explains to him why Hmong are in the US (*"It's a Vietnam thing. We fought on your side."*). Her openness wins Walt over who says *"You know something, kid? You're all right."* Sue explains that her brother Thao does not know which direction to go and that Hmong girls fit into American society more easily. *"The girls go to college, the boys go to jail"*. **relationships / education / crime**
	on their verandas	Walt, dog, Hmong grand-mother	Both, Walt and the Hmong grandmother, are on their verandas, holding their ground. Walt reads his birthday horoscope to his dog Daisy (*"This year, you have to make a choice between two life paths. Second chances come your way."*) poking fun at it. He watches Thao who goes and helps a white neighbour with her shopping bags. Thao's grandmother looks on proudly. **neighbourhood: parallel structure and characters / humour / surprise and approval / pride**
III. Parties and Families			
11	in Walt's home; same day	Walt, Mitch and Karen	**Unhappy Birthday** On his birthday, Mitch and Karen give Walt "useful" presents (a gopher and an oversized phone) and suggest him *"taking things easier"*. They have brought brochures of retirement homes and go on and on without realising that Walt resents their behaviour and their suggestions. He throws them out.
		Walt, Sue	When Sue invites him to come to their place for a barbecue as her special guest, he agrees. He has run out of beer and he says he *"might as well drink with strangers rather than drink alone"*. **family relations / isolation / sense of belonging**

12	at the Lors' house, same day	Sue, the Lor family and friends, shaman Kor Khue, Walt	**Not at Peace** Walt joins Sue who jokes *"when in Humong"*. Others are less friendly: Sue's grandmother is angry (yes, she hates him) and all gasp when he pats a little girl's head. Sue explains Hmong cultural rules and traditions to him. Walt notices the family witch doctor staring at him. Kor Khue "reads" him and says that people don't respect Walt and that Walt is not at peace because of something he did in the past. Walt is visibly upset and walks away. Sue, who follows him, sees that he has coughed up blood. Walt realises that he has *"a lot more in common with these gooks"* than with his own *"spoilt rotten family"*. **relationships / traditions / spirituality / understanding / illness**
13	same place, same day	Sue, Walt, Thao, Hmong guests, Youa	**Fixer and Toad** Walt, like a guest of honour, is being served Hmong food – which he likes. After a while, Sue takes him downstairs to mingle with the young generation. Walt notices a wobbly dryer and fixes it. He also notices that Thao keeps looking shyly at Youa who is on the sofa with some young men from Texas. He even catches Youa's glances at Thao. When Youa asks him what he does he explains that he fixes things. Walt lectures Thao – whom he calls Toad – on how to behave with girls and that he should not let Youa get away. **relationships / belonging / budding love**

Belonging I – Walt and Thao

14	at Walt's home; a day later	Walt, Hmong neighbours, Thao, Sue and their mother	**Making Amends** His Hmong neighbours bring Walt flowers and food – which he accepts and enjoys. Walt is being talked into accepting Thao's help. By working for Walt for a certain time, Thao will make amends for the attempted car theft. **relationships / neighbourliness**
15	around Walt's home	Walt, Thao	**Home Improvements** First, Walt does not give Thao any useful tasks; but then he realises that Thao can help neighbours maintain their neglected properties. Thoughtfully, Walt watches while Thao works hard. On his last day, Thao seems disappointed when Walt tells him he has done enough and should take the day off. Again, Walt coughs up blood. **relationships / achievement + satisfaction / illness**
16	at the hospital	Walt	**Nice Talking to You** At the clinic, Walt is bewildered, even slightly upset because there are multicultural patients and an assistant who mispronounces his name. His regular doctor has retired and has been replaced by an Asian doctor.
	on the phone with his son	Mitch	Back home after his medical appointment, he rings his son Mitch and asks about how everybody is doing, rather gravely. Mitch tells him if it isn't anything pressing Walt should call again some other time. Walt does not insist and hangs up; again he looks at his medical records, very gravely and sombrely.
	outside	Thao, Hmong gang	Walt sees the Hmong gang cruise past their houses; he aims his finger gun-like at them and mutters – thinking of Thao – that *"this kid doesn't have a chance"*. **bewilderment / family relations / loneliness / indifference / isolation / grave illness / preoccupation**

17	around the house	Walt Thao	**Helpful Hands** Walt does some minor repair work at the Lors' home. When Thao sees the tools in Walt's shed he states that he can never afford that. Walt gives him the basics to start with: WD-40 oil spray, vice grips and duct tape; he adds that Thao can borrow other tools he might need. Thao sees him cough up blood and is worried. When Walt has to ask for help with an old freezer, Thao asserts himself for the first time. Walt gives in, grumblingly.
		Sue	Sue thanks Walt for looking after her brother since *"he doesn't have any real role models in his life"* and calls "Wally" a *"good man"*. Walt does not want any thanks; he does not admit that he likes Thao, either. **relationships / neighbourliness / helpfulness / role models**
18	in Walt's garden	Walt, Thao	**Manning Thao Up** Walt asks Thao what he wants to do with his life. Thao is thinking about a career in sales, but studies will be expensive. So Walt suggests finding a job in construction (but before that he has to *"man up"* Thao, he says); he adds that Thao should ask "Yum-Yum" out.
	at the barber's	Martin	In order for Thao to learn *"how guys talk"* Walt takes him to see his friend Martin, the barber. Thao mangles it. **relationships / future / jobs / language**
19	at the construc-tion site;	Walt, Thao, foreman Tim Kennedy	**Construction Job** When meeting the foreman on the construction site, Thao makes good use of the hints he has been given by Walt and Martin. He is given a job.
	at DIY store; same day	Walt, Thao	Together, they buy equipment for Thao. Walt trusts Thao to *"pay him back on his first paycheck"*. Thao tells Walt that he really appreciates this. They shake hands, rather seriously. **jobs / language / confidence / trust**
Belonging II – The Gang			
20	way home from work	Thao, Hmong gang	**Making Him Look Bad** On his way home from work, although he asks them to leave him alone, Thao is attacked by the Hmong gang. They destroy his tools and burn his face with a cigarette while talking of *"saving face"*. Only reluctantly does Thao admit to Walt some days later what has happened. He does
		Walt	not want help, but appreciates the loan of some tools. **gangs / violence**
21	at the gang's house	Walt, Hmong gang	**Getting Ugly** Walt finds out where Thao's cousin and the gang live (Note the drum roll on the sound track!) He waits until the gang members leave, then rings the bell and beats up Smokie who opens the door. Before leaving, gun in hand, Walt tells him to tell the gang to stay away from Thao. Walt returns to his house; it's raining and a thunderstorm has started. **violence / intimidation**
	at Walt's place	Walt, the Lor family; Youa	Walt has invited his neighbours for a barbecue. Sue comments on his looking good and enjoying himself. When Walt hears that Thao has asked Youa out, he offers Thao the loan of the Gran Torino. **relationships / family / friendship / trust / well-being**

22	the Lors' house; at night	Walt, Hmong gang, the Lor family	**Targets** At night, the Hmong gang take revenge and open fire at the Lors' house in a drive-by shooting. Walt immediately runs over and checks on the family: Thao has a cut, but Sue is missing. Walt is devastated: *"In the war we lost a lot of friends but you're kind of set for it."* Sue is dropped off in front of her house, bloodied all over, barely able to walk. Seeing her, Walt drops his glass; her family weep. Sue does not say a word. **violence, intimidation, crime / relationships / sense of belonging / friendship / responsibility / war memories / trauma?**
23	at Walt's home, same night	Walt Father Janovich	**Pissed-Off Padre** Walt reproaches himself with what happened after he took the law in his own hands (*"you rotten fuck"*) and, in a blind rage, takes it out on his furniture. Then we see him in his chair, motionless, hands bloody, tears running down his face, his dog at his feet. Father Janovich finds Walt very calm and composed, his family photo album beside him. The priest says that none of the Hmong has been talking to the police. Walt knows that *"Thao and Sue are never going to find peace in this world as long as this gang is around."* Father Janovich calls the world *"unfair"*. They have a conversation – at eye level – about what should be done. Walt asks the priest to call him "Walt" and tells him he will find a solution. *"They don't have a chance."* **guilt / frustration / destruction / fear / vengeance / responsibility / relationships**
Life and Death and the Future			
24	at Walt's home, around town; next day	Walt, Thao	**What Needs to Be Done** Thao is burning to take revenge immediately, but Walt urges him to stay calm *"or else mistakes get made."* Thao begs Walt not to let him down. Walt tells him to go home and come back at four and promises that *"what needs to be done will be done"*. Walt sets his house in order: he mows the lawn; takes a bath; has a haircut and shave at his friend the barber's; and buys a bespoke suit. **relationships / planning and preparations**
25	in church; same day	Walt, Father Janovich	**At Peace** Walt confesses to Father Janovich that he kissed a woman not his wife in 1968, that he did not pay taxes on a $900 sale and that he never had a close relationship to his sons. Although the priest is sure that Walt left out what is really weighing him down, he absolves him. Outside the confessional, however, the priest tells him that he is going to the gang's house to prevent Walt from striking back and using violence. His *"Go in peace"* is countered by Walt's calm *"Oh, I am at peace"*, which really worries the priest. **relationships / (incomplete) confession**

26	in Walt's home; same day	Walt, Thao	**I Finish Things** Walt is cleaning his weapons when Thao enters. From his inexpert handling of the assault rifle it is clear that Thao has never used a gun before. Walt takes him downstairs, talks about Korea and gives his Silver Star medal to Thao because *"there is always a chance you don't come back"*. Thao wants to know from Walt how many men he killed in Korea. After locking Thao securely in his basement Walt tells him that he shot a young kid (*"just like you"*) who wanted to give himself up – and that he has been thinking of his guilt every single day of his life. Before he leaves, he calls Thao his friend and states that he is going to finish things.
		grand-mother, dog, Sue	Walt approaches Thao's grandmother. They both speak in their own language. Walt leaves his dog with her and walks away. He rings Sue and tells her to set Thao free, which she does.
	at the gang's house	Father Janovich	In front of the gang's house, Father Janovich implores the police patrol to stay longer otherwise *"there will be bloodshed"*. They don't. They take the priest with them. **relationships / full confession / trauma of war / guilt / friendship**
27	in front of the gang's house	Walt, Hmong gang	**I've Got a Light** Walt has arrived in front of Smokie's house. Members of the gang come out. Neighbours are watching while Walt trades insults with them. He aims his finger at them. Then he puts his cigarette in his mouth and asks them for a light. Reaching into his jacket he murmurs *"Hail Mary, full of grace"*. He pulls out his right arm fast, and is immediately pierced by bullets, with all gang members firing at the same time. From a bird's eye view we see Walt's lighter in his right hand; he is lying on his back, arms spread out, like Christ on the cross. **relationships / expiation of guilt / redemption / sacrifice**
28		police, Thao, Sue	**Last Rites and Wishes** The police prevent Thao from getting nearer. He finds out that the gang shot an unarmed man, that there are witnesses and that the gang members will go to prison for a long time. Sue and Thao, who is wearing Walt's Silver Star, watch silently as the gang are led away. **justice / friendship**
	in church	Vu, Sue, Thao, Father Janovich	In traditional costumes, Sue, Thao and their mother attend Walt's funeral. Father Janovich makes a very emotional speech which shows their mutual appreciation.
	at the lawyer's	Walt's family	At the reading of the will, Walt's family learn that his house goes to the church, and his Gran Torino to Thao. Walt's own family is not even mentioned. **relationships / appreciation / respect / bequests**
29	in the car	Thao and Daisy	**End Credits** In the final pictures (before the credits start to roll) we see Thao driving the Gran Torino, Daisy at his side, and hear the song Gran Torino (the first part of which is performed by Clint Eastwood) where we discern "Heart locked in a Gran Torino It beats a lonely rhythm all night long." and later "Do you belong in your skin Just wondering". **relationships / family / belonging**

While-viewing Activities – Gran Torino

Worksheet Part I a) Neighbours – Walt and the Hmong (Chapters 1+2)

Tasks:

1. During the first viewing take notes and present your first impressions:

   about Walt Kowalski
   about Walt Kowalski's family
   about the priest
   about the Hmong family next door
   about the relationship between the neighbours
   about Thao

2. Which topics do you spot?

3. Complete your notes during and after the second viewing.

Worksheet Part I b) Getting to know Thao (Chapters 3+4)

Tasks:

1. Take notes and present Thao

   – how he behaves at home
   – how he behaves towards the Latino gang
   – how he behaves towards his cousin and the Hmong gang on his way home
   – how he behaves towards "Spider", "Smokie" and the gang the next day

Homework Tasks:

1. Write a short summary of **The family gatherings** at the Kowalski home and at the Hmong family's home, pointing out differences and similarities.

2. Write a short essay about how you see **Thao's future**.

For the teacher:

Part I a) Neighbours: Walt and the Hmong

ad 1: First impressions about the characters.
about Walt Kowalski:
At his wife Dorothy's funeral and at the reception, he stands apart. Walt comes across as a person who is sour and embittered, old-fashioned but self-reliant. He coughs from time to time; he might be ill. He relates to his dog Daisy, however.
about Walt Kowalski's family:
His married sons and their families do not care about him; the young people are disrespectful and indifferent; the boys don't even talk to him; Ashley even wants to know what will happen to his vintage car when he dies; they all want to get home as soon as possible.
about the priest:
He is very young. Walt does not take him or what he says seriously. He insists the priest call him Mr Kowalski. Undeterred, the priest mentions Dorothy's wish for Walt to go to confession which Walt – ironically and impolitely – counters with "I confess that I have no desire to confess to a boy that's just out of the seminary".
about the Hmong family next door:
Their house looks run-down. People keep arriving bringing bowls of food. They speak an unknown Asian language. They behave in a friendly way.
about the relationship between the neighbours:
Walt is not helpful towards them and uses epithets. They do not interact.
about Thao:
The young man seems polite, but Walt uses racial slurs to send him away.

ad 2: The topics in this part are family relations; neighbourhood; racism; disrespect.

Part I b) Getting to know Thao

About Thao, how he behaves **at home**:
Thao washes the dishes and does everything his sister says; his grandmother thinks that he will never become the man in the house; Thao leaves during the celebration.

How he behaves towards **the Latino gang**:
Thao is walking down the sideway reading a book when the Latino gang rolls by and one person calls out to him asking whether he's a girl or a boy. They go on insulting him, but he keeps walking and does not react to their slurs.

How he behaves towards **his cousin and the Hmong gang**:
Thao's cousin "Spider", the driver of the Hmong gang's car, spots him. They frighten away the Latino gang because of their better artillery. They expect Thao to get into their car and to be thankful because they "bailed his ass out". But Thao keeps on walking until they block his way. Not even then does he get into their car. Before they drive away, "Smokie", the gang leader, tells him that they will get him the next day.

How he behaves towards **"Spider", "Smokie" and the gang the next day**
When the gang arrive the next day, Thao is weeding the garden. He tries to stay out of it, but his cousin and "Smokie" are insistent: he should roll with them. Reluctantly he finally gives in and asks what he has to do. He is to steal his neighbour's Gran Torino.

Suggested Answers for the Homework Tasks:

ad 1. Short summary of **The family gatherings**

The film **Gran Torino** starts with two family gatherings. One is in Walt Kowalski's house – it is the reception after his wife's funeral. Although many neighbours and friends and Walt's two sons and their families are present, Walt is not really included. The only person who seems to care about him is the priest, whom Walt rejects. Walt's sons mention that nothing can satisfy Walt and that that is the reason why they "don't do Thanksgiving" anymore. His grandchildren are disrespectful, uncaring and self-centred. His grand-daughter Ashley openly asks him what he plans to do with his vintage car when he dies; and she adds that she would like to have "the retro couch", too. They all leave as soon as possible and leave Walt to look after a guest's car battery.

There is also a family gathering in the house next door. Many guests arrive bringing bowls of food. A shaman is present and kills the sacrificial rooster. In a baptism ceremony he blesses the young woman and her baby. The guests, most of them in traditional clothing, mill around, like in Walt's house. The one person who stands out here is Thao – he is doing a girl's job by washing the dishes. His grandmother doesn't consider him man enough to head the family in the future.

In Walt Kowalski's home, the family has gathered because of a death and a funeral – the ending of a life. In the Hmong household, the family has come together because of a birth and a baptism, the beginning of a life.

ad 2. Short essay about **Thao's future**.

Judging from the scenes we have seen, Thao comes across as a polite, perhaps even timid young man. He does not look cool, he doesn't even behave cool – he is reading a book on his walk home from school. He lives in a household with his widowed grandmother, his widowed mother and his sister. His grandmother does not think he can fill the role of the man in the family because he does "woman stuff" like washing the dishes.

When his cousin Fong/Spider and the other gang members arrive to pick him up to roll with them, he is weeding the garden, doing a "woman's work" as his cousin states. Although Thao tries to stay out of it and Sue tells the gang members to leave him alone, they continue to put pressure on Thao until he finally asks what he has to do. He is to steal his neighbour's Gran Torino.

Thao is too weak to withstand the gang's pressure. He will steal the car and join the gang. He will become like his cousin Fong. In the future, the gang will be his family.

Worksheet   Part II a) Life and Death (Chapters 5+6)

Tasks:

1. Analyse Walt and the priest's attitudes and opinions in this scene. Refer to the extract.
2. Why can the heading "Life and Death" also be used for the scene in Walt's garage? Explain.

Extract from Chapter 5: (In the **V**eterans of **F**oreign **W**ars Bar, where Walt is with friends)

Father Janovich:	*Let's talk about something else.*
Walt:	*What?*
Father Janovich:	*Life and death.*
Walt:	*Life and death. What the hell do you know about life and death?*
Father Janovich:	*I'd like to think I know a lot. I'm a priest.*
Walt:	*Yeah. You get up and preach about life and death ... but all you know is what you learned in priest school. Right out of the Rookie Preachers Handbook.*
Father Janovich:	*I don't know about that. I think ...*
Walt (cuts him off):	*Death is bittersweet? Sort of bitter in its pain, but sweet in its salvation. That's what you know about life and death, and it's pathetic.*
Father Janovich:	*What do you know, Mr. Kowalski?*
Walt:	*I know a lot. I lived for almost three years in Korea with it. We shot men, stabbed them with bayonets, hacked seventeen-year-olds to death with shovels, for Christ's sake. Stuff I'll remember till the day I die. Horrible things, but things I'll live with.*
Father Janovich:	*And what about life?*
Walt has to think for a second. He struggles with his answer.	
Walt:	*Well, I ... I survived the war... got married ... had a family.*
Father Janovich:	*Sounds like you know a lot more about death than you do living.*
Walt downs a shot.	*Maybe so, Father. Maybe so.*

● **For the teacher:**

ad 1: Father Janovich is persistent and finds Walt and his friends in a veterans bar where they are trading racist jokes. When the priest starts his talk about life and death, Walt mockingly repeats the words from his eulogy and accuses him of not knowing anything about life and death because he is too young and too inexperienced.
When asked about what he knows, Walt recalls war experiences – horrible scenes where they cruelly killed 17-year-olds; he adds that he has to live with these memories. He is stymied, however, when asked about what he knows about life. He comes up with the weak answer that he survived the war, married and founded a family. The priest has hit a nerve – Walt reluctantly admits that he knows more about death than about living.

ad 2: When Walt hears noises in his garage and goes in, his gun at the ready, he faces young Thao. They both stumble, and Walt's bullet ends up in one of his beer signs on the wall. Thao gets away unharmed. This confrontation could easily have ended differently – with Thao dead on the ground. Nobody would blame Walt – he is allowed to use force to defend his ground.
(In addition to that, Walt's coughing up blood hints at a serious illness.)

Worksheet   Part II b) Defending One's Turf (Chapters 7-10)

Tasks:

1. Why do the gang come to the Lors' house? What happens?

2. A garden gnome gets broken. What could this symbolise?

3. When and how does Walt interfere? What makes the gang leave?

4. How do his neighbours and their friends react? What is Walt's answer?

5. How does Walt explain not calling the police? What does the priest think of this?

6. What does the priest suggest? Which insight does Walt offer?

7. From their talk, what do we guess about the relationship between Martin the barber and Walt?

8. Why do Sue and her date Trey get into an altercation with the black gang? What happens?

9. Walt says that he is a man they shouldn't fuck with. Then he points his fingers gunlike at them. What is their first reaction? When does that change?

10. What are Walt's reproaches to Sue? (See extract below) Why does he make them?

11. What does Sue explain to Walt about the Hmong and about her brother?

12. What does Walt's horoscope mean? (See extract below) How does Walt react?

13. What does he see Thao do? How does Thao's grandmother react?

ad 10: In the truck
WALT: *What's the matter with you, for Chrissake? Trying to get yourself killed? I thought you Asian girls were supposed to be smart. Hanging around a neighbourhood like that is a fast way to get you in the obituaries.*
SUE: *I know, I know, take it easy.*

ad 12: On the porch
WALT: *Your birthday today. This year you have to make a choice between two life paths. Second chances come your way. Extraordinary events culminate in what might seem to be an anti-climax.*

For the teacher:

1. Why do the gang come to the Lors' house? What happens?
   They come to pick up Thao to give him a second chance to become a member of their gang. When they want to drag him off by force, Sue and others join in the melee and try and free him.

2. A garden gnome gets broken. What could this symbolise?
   The garden gnome, which marked the border to Walt's property, gets smashed in the melee. Now he is part of the fight: his ground is being violated.

3. When and how does Walt interfere? What makes the gang leave?
   As soon as they are on his property, Walt stands his ground with his assault rifle and tells them to "get off". His fearless attitude makes the gang retreat.

4. How do his neighbours and their friends react? What is Walt's answer?
   The neighbours thank him, with words and the next day, with gifts of flowers and food. Walt does not want any of that; he wants to be left alone. He throws the food out. His explanation from the previous night – *"Get off my lawn"* (=respect my privacy) – holds.

5. How does Walt explain not calling the police? What does the priest think of this?
   Walt explains that in Korea, men had to react quickly. The priest points out that this is not Korea and that civil rules apply here.

6. What does the priest suggest? Which insight does Walt offer?
   The priest suggests it would do Walt good to *"unload some of the burden"* and find forgiveness. Walt points out that the things that haunt a man the most are the things he isn't order to do. (There must be a terrible secret which Walt does not want to talk about; something he did without being ordered to do it.)

7. From their talk, what do we guess about the relationship between Martin the barber and Walt?
   They know each other well; they are on friendly terms.

8. Why do Sue and her date Trey get into an altercation with the black gang? What happens?
   When the black gang members insult Sue Trey reacts as if he were black and addresses them as "bro". They become really aggressive and push him aside. Sue is defending herself when Walt stops his truck and intervenes.

9. Walt says that he is a man they shouldn't fuck with. Then he points his fingers gunlike at them. What is their first reaction? When does that change?
   First they think he is crazy and ridiculous; they don't take him seriously. But when he pulls out his pistol, they respect him and let Sue go.

10. What are Walt's reproaches to Sue? Why does he make them?
    That she has been risking her life by walking along in that neighbourhood and that her boyfriend or date is not very smart. Walt seems to care about Sue's well-being.

11. What does Sue explain to Walt about the Hmong and about her brother?
    Sue explains that Hmong people come from different parts of Laos, Thailand and China. They are here because they fought with the Americans in the Vietnam War and had to flee when the Communists came into power. Sue explains that her brother is really smart, but he lacks role models and doesn't know which direction to choose. Hmong girls adapt more easily to American culture. *"The girls go to college, the boys go to jail."*

12. What does Walt's horoscope mean? How does he react?
    It says that he has to make choices and that second chances come his way. He considers it *"a load of shit"* = he thinks it is ridiculous and far from the truth.

13. What does he see Thao do? How does his grandmother react?
    He sees Thao pick up a white neighbour's shopping. He realises that Thao is helpful and polite. Thao's grandmother has seen it, too. She nods proudly.

While-viewing Activities – Gran Torino

Worksheet   **Part III) Families and Parties** (Chapters 11-13)

Tasks:

1. Take notes about Walt's birthday and about the party at the Lors' home. Fill in the table. Watch out for how people behave towards Walt and how he reacts. Find a quotation to summarise each column.

At Walt Kowalski's home	At the Hmong family's home
Quotation	*Quotation*

2. Summarise what the shaman's message to Walt is.

3. What does Walt refer to when he says: *"I've got more in common with these goddamned gooks than my own spoiled-rotten family"*.

4. Point out why Walt's answer *"I'm fine"* is not true on two accounts.

5. How do the Hmong neighbours behave towards Walt after the party? What has changed?

Homework Task:

Find explanations for Walt's attitude towards his Hmong neighbours. In Chapter 7, he throws their food and their flowers into the bin; in Chapter 14, he accepts them, even gratefully (after a while).

For the teacher:

The filled-in table should contain the following:

At Walt Kowalski's home	At the Hmong family's home
Mitch and Karen arrive without their children. A store-bought cake is on the table. Their presents are gifts fitting for an immobile elderly person: a gopher and a phone with really big numbers. They tell Walt that he *"should think about taking it easier"*. Mitch tells him that he should give up smoking. They point out that it will be hard for him to maintain his house. That is why they have brought a large number of brochures of retirement homes – which are like *"holiday resorts"*, where he *"can meet other people"* like him, with shops where he *"can buy shoes"* and places where he *"can play golf"*.	Sue invites Walt over to their house as her special guest. They are having a barbecue. He joins them because he has run out of beer (and hasn't had much to eat, and probably because it is his birthday and he might want to be among some people). He says: *"Well, I might as well drink with strangers rather than drink alone."* Sue's grandmother hates Walt and doesn't want him among the guests. Walt commits the faux-pas of touching a child's head. Sue explains Hmong traditions to him and that he has to understand cultural differences to understand Hmong behaviour. Kor Khue, the Lor family shaman, has heard about Walt. He "reads" him and points out that Walt does not get respect and that he is not at peace because of something he did in the past.
Walt's anger increases and he throws them out.	Although Walt has coughed up blood after the "reading", he enjoys the food and the company.
It seems as if Mitch and Karen haven't even understood what upset him. Either they do not know him or they do not care. They disrespect his obvious wish to continue living in the house which he shared with his wife. They would probably like to sell it.	When asked about what he does he tells Youa that he "fixes things". Walt calls Thao a pussy and gives the shy and love-stricken young man the advice to go for the girl since she is interested in him. Walt adds that he knows about women because he *"got the best woman who was ever on this planet to marry"* him.
They have not shown any feelings towards the lonely bereft widower. They only think of themselves.	Walt has been included in this party (well, apart from grandmother). He feels understood by the shaman. He is treated well by the guests and Sue. He even fixes a dryer and gives advice to Thao.
"We miss mama, don't we, Daisy?"	***"I've got more in common with these goddamned gooks than my own spoiled-rotten family."***

In order to point out the differences one could use these two screenshots:
Birthday 1:   Walt in the middle, seated, over-towered by Mitch and his wife Karen (00:38:35)
Birthday 2:   Walt in the middle, seated, surrounded by Hmong women (00:46:48)

2. Summarise what the shaman's message to Walt is.

Kor Khue's "reading" of Walt.

(While Sue keeps translating the Hmong words Kor Khue says to him, Walt becomes quieter and quieter and more and more pre-occupied.)

SUE: *Kor Khue says people do not respect you. They don't even wanna look at you.*
        He says the way you live your food has no flavour. You're worried about your life.
        You made a mistake in your past life, like a mistake that you did, you're not satisfied with.
        He says you have no happiness in your life. It's like you are not at peace.
        (Walt stands up and walks away. When he starts coughing up blood he withdraws to a bathroom. He washes his face and looks into the mirror.)

WALT: *God, I've got more in common with these gooks than I do my own spoilt-rotten family.*

The shaman rightfully points out that Walt does not get any respect, that Walt made a mistake in the past and that that is the reason why Walt is not at peace.

3. What does Walt refer to when he says: *"I've got more in common with these goddamned gooks than my own spoiled-rotten family"*.
    This could summarise the experiences he has made on his birthday – from his calculating son and daughter-in-law to his more perceptive and even caring Hmong neighbours.

4. Point out why Walt's answer *"I'm fine"* is not true on two accounts.
    First of all, he is coughing up blood, which means he is seriously ill.
    Secondly, the shaman's words have hit a nerve. He is not at peace; there is something from his past that is niggling him. He does not feel happy.

5. How do the Hmong neighbours behave towards Walt after the party? What has changed?
    Again, they bring flower bouquets and food – but this time he accepts them.
    He says he likes the food better than beef jerky. But he has also realised that he likes to be part of a community and not stand alone.

Homework Task:

Find explanations for Walt's attitude towards his Hmong neighbours. In Chapter 7, he throws their food and their flowers into the bin; in Chapter 14, he accepts them, even gratefully (after a while).

Some might argue that Walt is ambiguous in his dealing with his neighbours. But a more straightforward explanation could be that Walt has commitment issues. He has difficulties in relating to people around him, especially to people with a different background and different customs. We remember his sons wondering at Dorothy's funeral service how Walt would get along in the "old neighbourhood". It has changed a lot since they were boys. Most of the houses of their neighbours, who were of Polish descent like Walt and his wife – Walt mentions Polarski, who lived next door – have been sold. Hmong people now live in them. We have also seen that Walt's relationship with his sons and their families is not close.

So Walt's throwing away all his Hmong neighbours' gifts in the first scene and later accepting the gifts and even gladly thanking his neighbours is less a sign of ambiguity than a sign of character development and towards committing.

From totally negating all contact with the neighbours, symbolised by his *"Get Off My Lawn"*, Walt has grown into being part of the neighbourhood (again) and liking it.

While-viewing Activities – Gran Torino

Worksheet   Part IV) Belonging I – Walt and Thao (Chapters 14-19)

Tasks:

1. Why do Walt and Thao get into closer contact?

2. Describe the development in the relationship between Walt and Thao. Use the conversation as a starting point.
   THAO: *So, what do you have for me today? You want me to watch paint dry? Maybe even count the clouds that pass by?*
   WALT: *Don't get flip with me, boy. I'm not the one who tried to steal. Don't you forget that.*
   THAO: *Go ahead. I don't care if you insult me or say racist things. Because you know what? I'll take it.*
   WALT: *Yeah, course you'll take it, because you have no teeth, you have no balls, kid.*
   THAO: *Look, I'm stuck here. So why don't you just find something useful for me to do?*

3. What do you think Walt wants to say to Thao when he calls him back saying *"Toad? – Nothing, never mind"*?

4. During his visit in the health clinic, what upsets and confuses Walt?

5. Why does Walt ring his son Mitch? How does this call go?

6. Why does Walt say *"This kid doesn't have a chance"*? What gesture does he make?

7. What does Thao really mean when he asks Walt about his tools? What does Walt do?

8. When Walt says *"My Gran Torino"* we see him smile, really smile, for the first time. Explain.

9. Explain Thao's behaviour in this scene, in which they are about to move Walt's freezer.
   THAO: *I'll take the top. It looks pretty heavy.*
   WALT: *Look, I'm not crippled. I've got the top.*
   THAO: *If you don't let me take the top, I ain't helping. I'll go back home.*
   WALT :   *Now, listen to me, zipper head ---*
   THAO: *No, you listen, old man. I'm here because you needed help, so it's either top or I'm out of here.*

10. a) What does Sue say about role models? What was their father like?

    b) What does Walt teach Thao according to Sue? Why?

11. What are Thao's plans for his future? What is the outcome of his conversation with Walt?

12. No need to discuss if the scene at the barber's is realistic. Just one question: Does Thao profit from it?

13. What is remarkable about when Walt and Thao buy equipment in the hardware store?

For the teacher:

1. Why do Walt and Thao get into closer contact?
    By trying to steal Walt's car, Thao dishonoured his family. That is the reason why Thao's mother Vu wants him to work for Walt to make amends for his attempted car theft.

2. Describe the development in the relationship between Walt and Thao. Use the conversation as a starting point.

THAO:	*So, what do you have for me today? You want me to watch paint dry? Maybe even count the clouds that pass by?*
WALT:	*Don't get flip with me, boy. I'm not the one who tried to steal. Don't you forget that.*
THAO:	*Go ahead. I don't care if you insult me or say racist things. Because you know what? I'll take it.*
WALT:	*Yeah, course you'll take it, because you have no teeth, you have no balls, kid.*
THAO:	*Look, I'm stuck here. So why don't you just find something useful for me to do?*

    Initially Walt refuses Thao's help, but he is talked into accepting him by Thao's mother and sister. Thao does not have any valid answer when asked what he is good at; so Walt doesn't give him anything worthwhile to do. But after this conversation, they find a means to work with each other: Walt makes him do repair work for Hmong neighbours while he watches him, thoughtfully. Thao works hard and relentlessly. Not only does Thao feel useful, but he also learns a lot about home improvement.
    Walt is very pleased with how his neighbourhood improves and with how Thao copes: Thao is getting better at repair and maintenance work. He seems to like the fact that he is needed. On his last day, he walks proudly up to Walt's door rubbing his calloused hands; Thao knows that he has risen to the task presented to him and mastered it. He cheerfully asks Walt for more work. He is quite disappointed when Walt gives him the day off.

3. What do you think Walt wants to say to Thao when he calls him back saying *"Toad? – Nothing, never mind"*?
    Probably something like "You have done good work." Because before that he told Thao that he has done enough. Also, Walt has watched Thao more and more approvingly.
    Walt has just coughed up blood; but he would not talk about his health problems with Thao.

4. During his visit to the health clinic, what upsets and confuses Walt?
    The clinic staff and the patients have become quite multicultural. He seems to be the only white person in the waiting room. Furthermore, the assistant wearing a headscarf pronounces his name as *"Koski"*; then there is a young Asian doctor because "his" doctor has retired three years ago. And then there is the doctor's worrying announcement about *"a full battery of tests"* to find out more about *"his issues"*.

5. Why does Walt ring his son Mitch? How does this call go?
    He certainly wants to talk to him about his health issues – he has all his files in front of him. At the top of one we can read "Hospital Admittance Form".
    First no one in Mitch's family wants to pick up the phone: Mitch does not really make time for Walt's preoccupation; he does not even realise that Walt wants to be asked how he is. Quite curtly, Mitch asks if it is anything pressing; Walt says no. So Mitch tells his father to ring some other time and they hang up.

6. Why does Walt say *"This kid doesn't have a chance"*? What gesture does he make?
    Again, the Hmong gang are riding by in their car. He sees them look at Thao, who is clearing the back yard, and at Thao's house.
    Walt's hand gesture of a gun being fired is answered with the middle finger by a gang member.

7. What does Thao really mean when he asks Walt about his tools? What does Walt do?
    Thao would like to do repair work, but he knows he cannot afford so many tools.
    Walt gives him the most important items: WD-40 oil spray, vice grips and some duct tape. He tells
    Thao that he can borrow anything else he might need.

8. When Walt says *"My Gran Torino"* we see him smile, really smile, for the first time. Explain.
    Walt seems to think it is funny that Thao, to whom he has become quite close, was to steal his Gran
    Torino as an initiation to the Hmong gang.

9. Explain Thao's behaviour in this scene, in which they are about to move Walt's freezer.
    THAO: *I'll take the top. It looks pretty heavy.*
    WALT: *Look, I'm not crippled. I've got the top.*
    THAO: *If you don't let me take the top, I ain't helping. I'll go back home.*
    WALT :   *Now, listen to me, zipper head ---*
    THAO: *No, you listen, old man. I'm here because you needed help, so it's either top or I'm out of here.*

    Thao has become assertive and holds his ground. He does not give in to Walt in this scene.

10. a) What does Sue say about role models? What was their father like?
    Sue thanks Walt for being a role model for Thao because he does not have any in his life. Sue adds
    that Walt is a good man and that she wishes their father had been more like him. He was very tradi-
    tional, very strict, very old-school. She thinks Walt being old-school is OK because he is American.

    b) What does Walt teach Thao according to Sue? Why?
    He teaches Thao how to repair things and he saved him from becoming a gang member. Sue is sure
    that he does it because he likes Thao.

11. What are Thao's plans for his future? What is the outcome of his conversation with Walt?
    Thao would like to go into sales. To achieve that, he has to go to college. But in order to afford that,
    he needs a job. So Walt promises to *"man him up"* and to procure him a job in construction. And he
    suggests Thao should ask Youa out.

12. No need to discuss if the scene at the barber's is realistic. Just one question: Does Thao profit from
    it?
    Yes, he does. Because he uses the sentences about costly car repairs, etc., in his conversation with
    the foreman and he secures the job.

13. What is remarkable about when Walt and Thao buy equipment in the hardware store?
    Walt picks out tools he knows Thao will need and he trusts Thao to pay him back once he earns
    money. Thao says that he really appreciates that and thanks Walt. Walt stretches out his hand – the
    two shake hands. As equals. (From now on, Walt will never again call him Toad.)

Homework Task:

Point out which values Sue appreciates in Walt. How does she deal with his racism and prejudices?

Sue emphasises that she considers Walt *"a good man"* (which he denies) because he looks after Thao – he cares about the young man's welfare and he is teaching him useful skills. Walt is a traditional American with old-school values (patriotism, reliability, honour).

She doesn't take Walt's racist remarks seriously, she even makes jokes, e.g., when she invites him to the party and mentions *"we only eat cats"*; or when Walt points out that *"only idiots"* want to live in the cold American Midwest, she laughingly thanks him for the ride. And she undeterredly calls him Wally.

While-viewing Activities – Gran Torino

Worksheet   Part V) Belonging II – The Gang (Chapters 20-23)

Tasks:

1. Describe Thao's mood and attitude as he walks home from work.

2. How do the gang members and Thao interact?

3. How does he deal with it when he meets Walt?

4. What does Walt do once he has found the gang's house?

5. Point out the significance of the thunderstorm.

6. Walt has invited the neighbours for a barbecue. Describe the atmosphere.

7. What happens at night?

8. What does Walt do when he gets home? How is he when the priest comes?

9. What is the outcome of the conversation between Walt and Father Janovich?

Homework Task:

Discuss Walt's interference and his responsibility for what happened to Sue. Take his monologue into consideration:
WALT: *Ah, Sue. I knew this was gonna happen. Tried to – What the hell am I doing here?*
         In the war, we just lost a lot of friends, but you're kind of set for it. You're geared to it.
Walking to his home, muttering *No, no, no. And then: You fuck! You rotten fuck!*

For the teacher:

1. Describe Thao's mood and attitude as he walks home from work.
   He looks pleased with himself.

2. How do the gang members and Thao interact?
   When the five gang members approach him, Thao does everything he can to avoid a confrontation. He asks them to leave him and his tools alone. But they become aggressive and break most of his tools. Then Smokie talks of "saving face" – Thao has made the gang look stupid and ineffectual because he didn't join – and presses a burning cigarette into his cheek. Thao yowls with pain.

3. How does he deal with it when he meets Walt?
   First he pretends that he has been busy; when Walt sees the wound Thao tells him that he can deal with it. Finally he tells Walt about the incident and says that he will replace his broken tools. Thao does not tell Walt where his cousin lives, saying he does not want Walt to interfere.

4. What does Walt do once he has found the gang's house?
   He waits till most gang members have left. Then he takes his pistol and approaches the door. He immediately attacks and beats up Smokie who opens the door. He tells him that they should leave Thao alone; otherwise they would have to deal with him and it would be "fucking ugly".

5. Point out the significance of the thunderstorm.
   Thunder and lightning serve as a premonition of something bad about to happen.

6. Walt has invited the neighbours for a barbecue. Describe the atmosphere.
   They are all at ease; Sue remarks that she has never seen Walt enjoying himself so much before. And when Thao and Youa tell him that they have a date, he offers them his Gran Torino to go out in style.

7. What happens at night?
   The Hmong gangbangers drive by and shoot at the Lors' house. Walt goes over to make sure they are all safe. Sue is not home and not at her aunt's either. She comes hours later, beaten up and bloody, unable to tell anything, barely able to walk. The family, and Walt, are devastated. Somehow, the way the grandmother looks at Walt, she seems to be thinking of Walt as the white devil.

8. What does Walt do when he gets home? How is he when the priest comes?
   He punches his fists into furniture and glass, as a way to deal with his frustration. With bloody knuckles and tears running down his face, he sits down; Daisy is nearby. When the priest comes, he is sitting in his dark living room; there are family photo albums on the table.

9. What is the outcome of the conversation between Walt and Father Janovich?
   Father Janovich tells Walt that no one has been giving evidence to the police. The Hmong are keeping their mouths shut. He adds that Sue and the others are scared. The priest gets worried when Walt tells him that Sue and Thao will never find peace until the gang go away forever.
   Father Janovich tells Walt that Thao wants vengeance. Walt says that he does not know yet what he will do, but that he will think of something, ending with the cryptic words "Whatever it is, they won't have a chance."

Homework Task:

Walt has realised that his beating up Smokie has caused this spiral of violence. Smokie did not stay out of it, as Walt advised him to do; instead he has retaliated with gunshots and rape. Furthermore, the gang's spreading of fear has worked – no one is talking to the police, the priest tells him.

Walt feels directly responsible for what happened to Sue. That is why, in his frustration, he curses himself and punches his fists into his furniture. Tears run down his face; he is upset and feels worthless.

But he seems to want to make good for it when he says to the priest that he will think of a solution.

One might argue that the gang would have come again anyway – Sue has always been quite outspoken and Thao has again resisted them.

But the gang's direct assault immediately after Walt's interference – after Thao asked him not to get involved! – brings it home to Walt that his using violence turned the gang's violence onto Sue.

He is responsible for his friends' well-being; he is responsible for Sue and for Thao.

Worksheet   Part VI) Life and Death and the Future (Chapters 24-29)

Tasks:

1. What does Walt do after he has sent Thao home?

2. a) What is the priest's reaction when Walt says that he has come for confession?
    b) What is Walt's confession to the priest?
    c) How does he react when the priest asks him if this is all?
    d) What should he do to expiate (to make amends for) his sins?
    e) What are Walt's words to the priest before he leaves?

3. a) What is Walt doing when Thao comes in? What does Thao do?
    b) Why does Walt say that he has something to show him? What is it?
    c) What does he confess to Thao who asks him what it is like to kill a man?
    d) Why will Walt go alone?

4. a) What does Walt do before he leaves?
    b) How does he confront the gang? What goes on around the gang's house?
    c) What happens after Walt asks if they have got a light?
    d) Describe the bird's eye view of fallen Walt. What does it resemble? (01:42:03)
    e) What is Thao told when he arrives?

5. a) Who is present at Walt's funeral?
    b) What does Father Janovich say in his eulogy?
    c) Who is present at the lawyer's office?
    d) Who does Walt bequeath his goods to?

6. What can one now state about Thao's future?

Homework Task:

Walt's horoscope mentions crossroads and second chances. Point out how this comes true.

For the teacher:

1. What does Walt do after he has sent Thao home?
    He meticulously mows the lawn so that his garden looks perfect. He then takes a bath (and enjoys the luxury of smoking a cigarette in the bath-tub – for the first time, as he apologises to Daisy). At his friend's barbershop he gets a haircut and a straight shave (which he has never had before); after that he goes and gets himself a bespoke suit, also for the first time in his life.

2. a) What is the priest's reaction when Walt says that he has come for confession?
    First Father Janovich thinks that Walt has done something bad. He asks Walt immediately what he has done. Later he worries about what Walt will do and that he will strike back.

b) What is Walt's confession to the priest?
   In 1968, he kissed a woman not his wife; he did not pay taxes on a sale; and he did not manage to have a close relationship to his sons.
c) How does he react when the priest asks him if this is all?
   He answers that this has bothered him for years. Not more.
d) What should he do to expiate (to make amends for) his sins?
   He should say ten 'Hail Marys' and five 'Our Fathers'.
e) What are Walt's words to the priest before he leaves?
   He tells him that he has much to do. He adds that he is at peace.

3. a) What is Walt doing when Thao comes in? What does Thao do?
   Walt is cleaning his pistol. Thao inexpertly picks up the assault rifle and asks which one he will use.
   b) Why does Walt say that he has something to show him? What is it?
   He shows him his Silver Star medal and gives it to him because "there is always a chance you don't come back." But this has been a ruse to lure Thao to the basement and to lock him in there – he is not going to take Thao with him to confront the gang.
   c) What does he confess to Thao who asks him what it is like to kill a man?
   Walt confesses that, when they attacked an enemy machine-gun nest in 1952, he killed a young man who wanted to give himself up. As he was the only one who came back he was awarded the medal for bravery – which he considers the worst of it.
   d) Why will Walt go alone?
   Walt says that he thinks of that every single day as he has innocent blood on his hands. He will go alone because Thao has his whole life ahead of him; no killing should spoil his future.

4. a) What does Walt do before he leaves?
   He takes over his dog to the Hmong family and fixes the leash to the grandmother's chair leg. Then he rings Sue and tells her that Thao is in his basement and that she should free him.
   b) How does he confront the gang? What goes on around the gang's house?
   He walks up to the house and insults the gang members. He speaks up for Thao, then points his fingers at them and pretends to shoot them.
   Around them, other Hmong follow the confrontation.
   c) What happens after Walt asks if they have got a light?
   He starts saying *"Hail Mary, full of grace"* and, from his inner pocket, he pulls out his lighter, really fast. He is riddled with the gangbangers' bullets.
   d) Describe the bird's eye view of fallen Walt. What does it resemble? (01:42:03)
   We see Walt, on his back, both his arms stretched out from his body. Like Christ on the cross. This is Walt's way of expiating for his sins: by sacrificing himself he gives his friends a future.
   e) What is Thao told when he arrives?
   That "he" was shot when he took out his lighter, "he" was unarmed, that there are witnesses and that the gangbangers will go to prison for a long time.
   The last item we see in this scene is Walt's Silver Star medal on Thao's T-shirt.

5. a) Who is present at Walt's funeral?
   There is Walt's family and friends like Martin the Barber and acquaintances; Sue and Thao, in traditional Hmong clothes, and their mother Vu are among the mourners, together with more Hmong neighbours.
   b) What does Father Janovich say in his eulogy?
   He quotes Walt's outspoken words. He goes on to say that he knew nothing about life or death until he met Walt, who taught him a lot.
   c) Who is present at the lawyer's office?
   They are all present: all Walt's family, even all the grandchildren. And Thao.

d) Who does Walt bequeath his goods to?
   He leaves his house to the church; and his Gran Torino to Thao; not one item to his family.

6. What can one now state about Thao's future?
   In the last sequence, we see Thao driving the Gran Torino along the lake front, Daisy on the passenger seat. They look happy. They belong. Thao will have a future in America.

Homework Task:

Walt's horoscope mentions crossroads and second chances. Point out how this comes true.

On his birthday, Walt accepts Sue's invitation to the Hmong party. This is the beginning of his getting to know them better. At first reluctantly, he teaches Thao about house repair and maintenance and helps him find a job. He finds understanding and happiness with his Hmong neighbours. But in starting the spiral of violence to protect Thao from the gang, he sees Sue badly hurt. With his decision to confront the gang unarmed and to sacrifice himself, he expiates his sin of shooting the young Korean who wanted to give himself up, and of endangering Sue. Walt gives his life to secure a safe future for Thao and for Sue. He has taken the second chance that he was given by life and has redeemed himself.

While/Post-viewing Activities – Gran Torino

Worksheet   Recalling the Film 1 – Quotations

Task:

With your partner, discuss the quotations and point out the context in which people say the lines.

1. *"No, you listen, old man. It's either top or I'm out of here."*
2. *"Nothing is fair, Father."*
3. *"I am at peace."*
4. *"This kid doesn't have a chance."*
5. *"I'm proud to say that you are my friend."*
6. *"The girls go to college and the boys go to jail."*
7. *"Call me Walt."*
8. *"Speaking of busy, I got a lot on my plate right now, so if there's not something pressing ..."*
9. *"I fix things."*
10. *"Come back here at four this afternoon. And what needs to be done will be done."*
11. *"I'd let you take the Gran Torino."*
12. *"This is gonna end today."*

For the teacher:

1. *"No, you listen, old man. It's either top or I'm out of here."* Thao asserts himself for the first time, to Walt, when they move the freezer. (01:05:32)

2. *"Nothing is fair, Father."* Walt to the priest about the gang who raped Sue. (01:29:06)

3. *"I am at peace."* Walt to the priest, after his incomplete confession (01:34:31)

4. *"This kid doesn't have a chance."* Walt, about Thao, when seeing the gang drive by. (01:01:29)

5. *"I'm proud to say that you are my friend."* Walt to Thao, after he has locked him up. (01:37:10)

6. *"The girls go to college and the boys go to jail."* Sue to Walt, when he gives her a ride home after he has rescued her from the Latino gang. (00:36:42)

7. *"Call me Walt."* to the priest when he comes and sees him after Sue was raped. On all previous occasions Walt protested when the priest addressed him as Walt. Now he offers the familiar term of address. He feels the priest and he are on an equal footing. (01:29:17)

8. *"Speaking of busy, I got a lot on my plate right now, so if there's not something pressing ..."* Mitch to his father when Walt wants to talk to him about his illness and hospitalisation. (01:00:26)

9. *"I fix things."* During the party at the Hmong home, to Youa when she asks Walt about his occupation. (00:49:35) – Before he confronts the gang, he says to Thao *"I finish things"*.

10. *"Come back here at four this afternoon. And what needs to be done will be done."*
    Walt to Thao in the morning. But when Thao comes at four, eager for revenge, Walt locks him up before he leaves to confront the gang. (01:30:35)

11. *"I'd let you take the Gran Torino."* Walt to Thao who plans a date with Youa. (01:22:35)

12. *"This is gonna end today."* Thao, who wants immediate vengeance and who is upset that Walt says they have to stay calm and think before they act. (01:30:09)

While/Post-viewing Activities – Gran Torino

Worksheet   Recalling the Film 2 – Plot and Characters

Tasks:

With your partner, use the headings to point out the plot development. Mention what and who has changed in the course of the film, what and who has stayed the same.

1. **From funeral to funeral**

2. **Daisy – from porch to porch**

3. **a) Walt's Silver Star medal – from "hidden in a drawer" to "out into the open"**

    b) Walt's Zippo lighter

4. **Walt's Gran Torino – from "hidden in the garage" to "out into the open"**

For the teacher:

1. From funeral to funeral

The film starts with Dorothy's funeral, Walt Kowalski's wife; and it ends with Walt Kowalski's funeral.

Walt's family have not changed.
At Dorothy's funeral the children behaved tastelessly and were dressed inappropriately. The sons and their wives didn't show emotions and were seated far away from Walt.
Now they assist at Walt's funeral ceremony indifferently. However, at the lawyer's office, they expect to be considered in Walt's will. This does not happen: the house goes to the church *"because Dorothy would have loved it"*, his vintage car to his *"friend Thao Vang Lor"*.

The priest, in his eulogy, says that he has learned a lot from outspoken Walt. In the months between the two funerals they have become friends.

Again and again, Walt insisted that Father Janovich call him Mr. Kowalski and he rejected Father Janovich's "meddling". But when they have a beer together and talk about Thao and Sue and about them not having a chance of a peaceful life "if the gangs don't go away", he asks the priest to call him Walt. He trusts him and sees him as an equal – no longer as the *"overeducated, 27- year-old virgin"* *"who holds the hands of superstitious old women and promises them eternity"*.

Walt and the Lor family have become friends: Thao, Sue and their mother Vu assist at the funeral in their ceremonial Hmong clothing; Thao, in addition to that, has pinned on Walt's Silver Star medal. They are real and sincere mourners. Even grandma on her porch is quite subdued and solemn.

2. Daisy – from porch to porch

We first meet Daisy when Walt takes her out to his porch, pets her and talks to her, as if she were a person, during the funeral reception for Dorothy: *"We miss Momma, don't we, Daisy"*.

Daisy can be seen as a symbol of Walt's shifting trust and friendship towards the Hmong family.

Walt confides his worries to Daisy (instead of to his sons); Daisy is next to him when he cries for Sue. He even apologises to her for smoking in the house.

Before he leaves for his final encounter with the Hmong gang, he goes over to the Lors' house and hands his dog over to the reluctant grandmother. He tells Daisy to stay and he fixes her leash to the old lady's rocking-chair while she murmurs unkind things in Hmong. Here will be Daisy's new home.

Daisy is on the porch with grandmother when Thao, Sue and their mother leave for the funeral service. She belongs.

In the closing credits, we see Thao driving the Gran Torino, Daisy sitting beside him, her ears flapping.

3. a) Walt's Silver Star medal – from "hidden in a drawer" to "out into the open"

A Silver Star Medal is given to a soldier who has behaved heroically: it is awarded for "Gallantry in action against an enemy of the United States." It is the third-highest personal decoration for valour in combat.

During the funeral reception, Walt's bored grandchildren go through his belongings. The boys find his war decoration in a basement cupboard. They comment on it; but when Walt comes down into the basement, they do not ask him about his medal or about his war experience. They pretend to be just there, sitting next to each other on the sofa.

In the scene with Thao, when Thao is burning to go and shoot the Hmong gang, it is Walt who uses his Silver Star to lure Thao down into the basement and to talk about war experiences. Walt locks Thao in and only then does he answer Thao's question what it is like to kill a man.
"You want to know how it feels to kill a man? It feels goddamned lousy. And it feels even worse when you get a medal for bravery right after you mowed down some scared kid when he tries to give up. A dumb, scared, little gook, just about your age. I shot him with the same rifle you just held upstairs.
I've thought about that kid for fifty years. And I promise you, boy, you want no part of it. Me, I've got blood on my hands. I'm soiled. (This is the confession which Walt did not make to Father Janovich.) *Forgive me for tricking you like a dope. I'll call someone and have them let you out later."* Before leaving Walt says to Thao that he is proud to call him a friend. *"You have your whole life ahead of you."*

When Thao arrives at the gang's house with Sue, we see that he has Walt's medal pinned to his shirt.

Again he is wearing it at Walt's funeral. It now openly states Walt's bravery, whereas Walt kept it hidden. Walt felt ashamed and tormented because he was given it for bravery after he was the only one who came back after a suicidal attack in Korea in 1952; an attack in which he killed a boy who wanted to give himself up.

We remember Walt who says to his neighbours (who bring gifts after he rescued Thao) that he doesn't want to be a hero. By sacrificing himself so that Thao can live he has paid for the young Korean's death and has become a hero.

3. b) Walt's Zippo lighter

The emblem is the First Cavalry emblem. He has had it since 1951 when he was fighting in Korea in the First Cavalry. – This is the "gun" he pulls when facing the gang. When Walt is lying on his back ripped up by shots everyone can then see it in his open hand.

4. Walt's Gran Torino – from "hidden in the garage" to "out into the open"

Walt has been working in a Ford plant for 50 years "on the belt", as he says to Thao. He put the steering column into his Gran Torino in 1972. He is proud of his car and the American values it stands for.
The car is sitting under dust covers in his garage, when Ashley walks in during the funeral reception. She uncovers it. Walt finds her when she has a secret smoke next to the car. He puts out her cigarette and covers up his car again while Ashley compliments him on his cool car – which she likes! - and she pointedly asks him what will happen to the car once he dies. Walt is disgusted.
When Thao is in the garage to steal the car, the focus is on Thao and on Walt; the car is in the background.

But after that attempt, Walt polishes it and leaves it in his driveway all day and night. It is temptingly in the open.

In another scene Thao and Walt are in the garage again. Walt is repairing Thao's fan and faucet. When Walt enquires about the gang and the initiation ceremony, Thao points towards the Gran Torino in the driveway – which makes Walt smile broadly.

Even Tim Kennedy, with whom Walt has found a job for Thao, jokingly asks for the keys of the Gran Torino.

After that, we see Thao wash and polish the Gran Torino; and Walt and Sue commenting on it.

When they have a barbecue together and Thao admits that he has invited Youa on a date, Walt offers his Gran Torino so that they can go out in style.

In the scene in the lawyer's office, when the lawyer reads Walt's will, Ashley looks quite expectantly when Walt's Gran Torino is mentioned. However, it will go to Walt's *"friend Thao"*. Walt's family does not get one single item and is not even mentioned in his will.

In the final scene, we see Thao driving the Gran Torino with Daisy sitting beside him. They are enjoying the ride. They both belong.

While/Post-viewing Activities – Gran Torino

Worksheet   Recalling the Film 3 – Relationships

Tasks:

1. What's in a name?
Point out when and by whom the various forms of address are used and what they mean. Point out how, when or if they change.

Walt – Mr Kowalski – Wally – Koski

Thao – Toad

Sue – Dragon Lady

Fong – Spider

2. Belonging: society, ethnicity, culture, family, religion/beliefs, (peer) group, (linguistic) group, (age) group, (occupational) group, (political) party ....   and Identity

Point out to which group(s) the main characters belong and how this shapes their identity.

Walt

Thao

Sue

3. Gangs and Belonging

Use examples from the film to prove (or disprove) Spider's statement that gangs are family.
Start with this extract:

SMOKIE:	*Come on, ride with us. Chill with us.*
FONG/SPIDER:	*You need somebody to protect you, man. That's what your big coz is for.*
SMOKIE:	*Look dog. I been there, done it and I seen it, man. Back in the day, everybody used to wanna beat me up. But now, nobody wanna fuck with me.*
FONG/SPIDER:	*Come on. We're coz, right? We're family.*
SMOKIE:	*Look, a brother to Spider is a brother to me. Come on.*
THAO:	*So, what do I have to do?*
SMOKIE:	*Spider told me that our boy next door got a bad-ass whip.*
FONG/SPIDER:	*Come on. Nice. Yeah, my little cousin being a little man.*

For the teacher:

1. What's in a name?
Point out when and by whom the various forms of address are used and what they mean. Point out how, when or if they change.

Walt – Mr Kowalski – Wally – Koski
Walt insists the priest call him Mr. Kowalski until they get close after the attack on Sue. Then Walt asks Father Janovich to call him Walt. (However, in the church, when Walt comes for confession, the priest addresses him as Mr. Kowalski.)

Sue: *"Happy birthday, Wally"* when asking him over for their barbecue.

Sue: *"You are a good man, Wally"* when watching Thao washing Walt's Gran Torino). Walt does not want to be called Wally, but Sue does not care. She even calls him *"white devil"* jokingly during their barbecue. The new assistant in his health clinic cannot pronounce Kowalski and says Koski instead, which irritates Walt; the doctor pronounces his name correctly, however.

Thao – Toad

Walt calls Thao Toad although Thao protests. Walt addresses him as Toad even when he asks him for help with the freezer. Even Sue calls Thao Toad when they watch him washing Walt's car.

In using this denigrating term Walt shows that he thinks Thao is too sissy, "not man enough".

But after Walt has seen Thao's efforts to make amends – in which Thao did a lot to improve the neighbourhood – Walt extends his hand to Thao (in the hardware store). He shows that he appreciates Thao – their relationship has changed. From then on, Walt calls him Thao. Later he even says out loud that he is proud to call Thao his friend.

Sue – Dragon Lady

Walt calls her that in the car, after he rescued her from the Latino gang; and again at their barbecue in Walt's garden. He appreciates Sue; for him this is a term of endearment – countered by Sue's *"white devil"*.

Fong – Spider

Fong insists on being called Spider because that is his gang name. He has a spider tattoo to go with the name. Sue ridicules him for it.

2. Belonging: society, ethnicity, culture, family, religion/beliefs, (peer) group, (linguistic) group, (age) group, (occupational) group, (political) party .... and Identity

Point out to which group(s) the main characters belong and how this shapes their identity.

Walt

- American patriot (flag, gun, etc.) of Polish descent;
- Korean War veteran; (war memories or similar situations in the film are accompanied by drum rolls); he knows that he was given the medal for bravery for the wrong reasons. He does not consider himself a hero.
- He worked at a Ford Plant in Detroit all his life and is proud of his Gran Torino in which he himself mounted the steering column; he cannot understand his son who works for a Japanese dealership. Walt promotes blue-collar values.
- Although belonging to the Catholic Church, he is not a believer, he even mocks Father Janovich: When asked why he didn't call the police, Walt says *"I prayed for them to show up, but guess what? No answer."*
- He is an independent spirit and is used to dealing with a situation himself, but after his wife's death he is lonely since he has never managed to build a close relationship to his sons. He rebukes the priest who offers him a home in the religious community (The priest offers to hear his confession and give him forgiveness.).
- Again and again he fights against his Hmong neighbours' advances who want to thank him for looking out for Thao until he finally gives in and meets them, and eventually employs Thao. He states that he feels more at home with them than with his own family.
- He is left alone with his illness – his son does not let him talk; and Walt is too reticent to mention it to his Hmong neighbours or to the priest.

→ Walt Kowalski is presented as a distrustful, racist loner with good work ethics, an "old school American" – in Sue's words – who slowly changes towards a more caring person due to Sue and to his own involvement with Thao and the Hmong family.

Thao

- around 16, of Hmong descent, lives with his widowed mother and his older sister Sue and their grandmother next door to Walt.
- The Hmong are in the U.S. because of their alliance with the U.S. in the Vietnam War; Hmong came as refugees when the Communists took over. Although they fought with the U.S. forces, Walt links them to the "gooks" he fought in Korea and uses racial slurs when talking to them or about them.
- Their house looks neglected, appliances are falling apart. There is obviously not enough money or knowledge for maintenance.
- Not even by his own grandmother is Thao considered "the man in the house". He washes the dishes and does everything his sister tells him to do. Later we see him mulching the garden.
- He is quite shy, which we see when he first does not dare to approach Youa.
- He is well-behaved; he asks Walt politely about his help; he deals with Walt's racial slurs and he helps a white neighbour when her shopping bag rips.
- Thao likes reading and is a good student, but he lacks role models, Sue says. Sue adds that girls find it easier to adapt to American society than boys. *"Girls go to college, boys go to jail"*. We see this aspect when Thao is pressured by his cousin to join their gang. For Fong/Spider, Smokie and the others, the gang is their "family", where they belong.
- However, after his mangled initiation, he resists the gang's pressure.
- When made to work for Walt, Thao discovers that he has marketable skills in maintenance and construction. He realises that he is good at it and feels a sense of achievement. He can now earn some money towards his college education. He would like to have a career in sales.
- Left to his own devices, upset and vengeful Thao would fall into the trap of answering violence by violence. He is made to see that taking a life leaves a scar on a man's soul. Walt spares him this experience – he locks him in and confronts the Hmong gang alone.
- Walt and Thao have become friends. Thao has found an approach to the American way of thinking, a role model and probably even a hero. When Thao, Sue and their mother, in their traditional Hmong clothes, assist at Walt's funeral service, Thao has pinned Walt's medal for bravery to his shirt.

→ With the bequest of Walt's car, Thao has visibly arrived in American society, as we can see in the final pictures: Thao driving the Gran Torino, Daisy by his side.

Sue

- Thao's older sister; of Hmong descent
- Sue has already found her role: she is adapting to American society. She does not deny her Hmong roots, either, e.g. when she attends Walt's funeral in traditional clothing.
- She is very outspoken (sometimes even dangerously so) and straightforward. She is neither timid nor shy. Her behaviour is certainly more stereotypically American than Asian.
- She is strong and self-reliant, but also insightful and reliable.
- She watches over Thao (for example, when the Hmong gang come for him), tells Thao what to do and guides him.
- Sue is also the person who reaches out to Walt: She is undeterred by his grumpiness and his racial slurs and manages to draw Walt out of his shell when she invites him to their party. There, Walt's inner turmoil is "read" by the shaman who reveals that Walt is not at peace. Sue acts as an "interpreter" of Hmong language, behaviour and customs; but she is also the "facilitator" of the relationship between Walt and Thao. She (and her mother) make sure that Thao works for Walt to "pay off his debt" = to make amends for trying to steal the Gran Torino.

→ She is the link between Walt's American world and Thao, who is searching for a sense in his life and a place where he can belong.

3. Gangs and Belonging

Use examples from the film to prove (or disprove) Spider's statement that gangs are family.
Start with this extract:

SMOKIE:	*Come on, ride with us. Chill with us.*
FONG/SPIDER:	*You need somebody to protect you, man. That's what your big coz is for.*
SMOKIE:	*Look dog. I been there, done it and I seen it, man. Back in the day, everybody used to wanna beat me up. But now, nobody wanna fuck with me.*
FONG/SPIDER:	*Come on. We're coz, right? We're family.*
SMOKIE:	*Look, a brother to Spider is a brother to me. Come on.*
THAO:	*So, what do I have to do?*
SMOKIE:	*Spider told me that our boy next door got a bad-ass whip.*
FONG/SPIDER:	*Come on. Nice. Yeah, my little cousin being a little man.*

We see the gang defend their turf and intervene when Thao is bothered by the Latino gang.
But:
If gangs behaved like family, they would look out for others around them and not hurt them. There are multiple examples in which Thao is put under pressure and hurt until the horrific scene when Sue is raped.
The "gang family" only cares for gang members.

* * *

Research Task:

Go to the Official Site of The LOS ANGELES POLICE DEPARTMENT
http://www.lapdonline.org/get_informed/content_basic_view/1396
Present information on gangs in L.A.

For the teacher:

The County and City of Los Angeles are the "gang capital" of the nation. There are more than 450 active gangs in the City of Los Angeles. Many of these gangs have been in existence for over 50 years. These gangs have a combined membership of over 45,000 individuals.

During the last three years, there were over 16,398 verified violent gang crimes in the City of Los Angeles. These include 491 homicides, nearly 7,047 felony assaults, approximately 5,518 robberies and just under 98 rapes. Approximately half of the homicides are gang-related.

* * *

The following might be an interesting topic for a student presentation:

Stanley "Tookie" Williams (1953-2005)

In **Gangs and Wanting to Belong** (1996), he speaks out against gang violence.
Stanley "Tookie" Williams, cofounder of the Crips in Los Angeles, wrote this book while on Death Row in San Quentin, California for four murders.

His appeal for clemency was rejected by Gov. Arnold Schwarzenegger; "Tookie" was executed by lethal injection in 2005.

The film ***"Redemption: The Stan Tookie Williams Story"*** (USA 2004, 94 minutes) portrays his life.

While-viewing Activities – Gran Torino

Worksheet   The Language of Film

Task:

Work in groups.

In twos or threes, play-act the terms as stills.

Which camera angles would you use to show the following moods and characteristics?

> power
> humiliation
> idolisation/adoration
> threat
> superiority
> inferiority
> oppression
> helplessness
> dominance
> indifference
> appeal/pleading

Refer to the table below.

When to you use which angle, which shot

What?	Why?
Establishing shot: e.g. a long shot and a slow pan	to show the location at the start of a scene
Long shot: people/objects shown from a distance	for orientation; presents the entire setting
Medium long shot: subject of shot, e.g. a couple, is shown with surroundings	presents characters in setting
Full shot: shot of the whole body/object	presents a character or an object
Medium shot: upper body, part of an object	gives more details of character or object
Close-up: e.g. head and shoulders	to draw attention to s.o./s.th., to show nuances in expressions
Extreme close-up/detail shot: e.g. face only, or a detailed shot of an object	to point out particular importance of s.o./s.th.
Point-of-view shot (POV): shows the scene from the point of view of a character	to show the scene through the character's eyes so that the viewer can get emotionally and intellectually involved with the character
Over-the-shoulder shot (O.S.): parts of both characters in the dialogue are in the frame, the partner of the person speaking is seen over the speaker's shoulder	to imitate the attitude of an observer and to enhance the depth of a shot, to give spatial continuity by establishing the relative positions of each character

Reverse-angle shot: a shot from the opposite side	to give a different viewpoint (often used in dialogues)
To pan left/right: horizontal movement	to give a wider impression of the location
To tilt up/down: vertical movement	to show so./s.th. in full length
Canted angle = Dutch angle: a view in which the frame is not level	to give the impression of a loss of control or a sense of imbalance
To zoom in on s.o./s.th/out of s.o./s.th.: by adjusting the focal length during a shot	to concentrate on s.o./s.th./to move away from s.o./s.th.
Tracking (trucking) shot, dolly shot: the camera is mounted on a dolly, running on a track	to allow smooth and silent camera movements
Travelling shot: the dolly-mounted camera moves alongside the person/object	to give a sideways view of the person/object
to dolly in/to move in/to track in: to dolly out/back/to move out/to track back: by using a dolly-mounted camera	to move toward s.o./s.th. to show more details; to move away from s.o./s.th. to reveal more (This is not zooming!)
Eye-level shot: filmed at the level of a person's eyes, straight-on angle	no special function, ordinary, conventional, neutral – often used to convey the idea of authenticity, realism, objectivity
Low-angle shot: from below	to enlarge, to make more impressive
Below shot: from very much below, worm's eye view	to exaggerate the volume and importance of the person/object
Overhead shot: bird's eye view	to give an impression of the action/setting
High-angle shot: from above	to make s.o./s.th. seem small, weak
Crane shot: camera mounted on a crane to allow both horizontal and vertical movement	to allow dynamic and fast changes, to quickly reveal a very large space; the camera appears to move freely in the space above ground

Hitchcock's Rule:
In 1962, in his famous discussions with François Truffaut, Alfred Hitchcock coined this cinematographic principle stating that the size of an object in the frame should equal its importance in the story at the moment.

For the teacher:

The DVD-ROM *Close-up Exploring the Language of Film*[2] with extracts from over 150 films offers tutorials about film language, trains awareness when watching films and offers a variety of tools for analysing films and stills.

---

2 Close-Up Exploring the Language of Film Lernsoftware DVD-ROM, hrg. von Carola Surkamp, Schönigh, 2010

Further Task:

Work in groups.
Use your mobiles/your cameras to film this short sequence from various angles (high angle/low angle/straight-on angle; etc.).
Show and explain your results. Then point out how the scene is done in the film **(1:05:08 – 1:05:38)**.

In Walt's Basement
Walt and Thao are looking at the freezer strapped to the dolly.
WALT: Here's the deal. I take the top because that's the heaviest. I pull on that, and you stand
          right back here and you push and help me push it up each step. Just like that.
THAO: Then let me take the top. [...]
WALT: Look, I'm not crippled. I've got the top.
THAO: If you don't let me take the top, I ain't helping. I'll go back home.
WALT: Now listen to me, zipper head ...
THAO: No, you listen, old man. I'm here because you needed help. So it's either top or I'm out of here.

Homework Task:

Revise the vocabulary below. Then write a short statement about your viewing habits. Mention your favourite films/series, where they are set and which cinematographic means they use.

Useful Vocabulary Related to the Cinema/Movies

Watching
- to go to/take s.b. to (see) a film/movie
- to go to/sit in (BE) the cinema/(AE) the (movie) theatre
- to rent a film/movie/DVD
- to download a film/movie/video
- to burn/copy/rip a DVD
- to see/watch a film/movie/DVD/video/trailer/preview
- a cineast = a person who is enthusiastic about films and knows a lot about films

Showing
- to show/screen a film/movie
- to promote/distribute/review a film/movie
- to be on at the cinema (BE)
- to be released on/come out on/be out on DVD
- to captivate/delight/grip/thrill the audience
- to do well/badly at the box office
- to get a lot of hype/live up to the hype

Film-making
- to write/co-write a film/movie/script/screenplay
- to direct/produce/make/shoot/edit a film/movie/sequel/video
- to make a romantic comedy/a thriller/an action movie
- to do/work on a sequel/remake
- to film/shoot the opening scene/an action sequence/footage (of s.th.)

- to compose/create/do/write the soundtrack
- to cut/edit (out) a scene/sequence
- to fade in/fade out/to dissolve/fade to black/over black/fade up
- to close on/extremely close on
- to angle on
- Int. (= Interior): set indoors / Ext. (= Exterior): set outdoors
- shot: a piece of film that has been exposed without cuts or interruptions; a shot might be of any duration, from a fraction of a second to minutes or even hours.
- scene: a series of interrelated shots in a narrative film evoking the impression of continuous action that usually takes place in a single time and place, often with the same characters; the end of a scene is often indicated by a change in time, action and/or location.
- sequence: made up of several interrelated scenes
- to storyboard: to outline the story of a film/movie in a series of drawings or pictures (= storyboard)
- voice over (V.O.): the voice of the narrator/a character is heard while other sounds continue
- subtitle
- (inserted) caption

Acting
- to have/get/do an audition
- to get/have/play a leading/starring/supporting role
- to play a character/James Bond/the bad guy
- to act in/appear in/star in a film/movie/remake
- to do/perform/attempt a stunt
- to work in/make it big in Hollywood
- to forge/carve/make/pursue a career in Hollywood

Describing Films
- the camera pulls back/pans over s.o./s.th./zooms in (on s.o./s.th.)
- the camera focuses on s.o./s.th./lingers on s.o./s.th.
- to shoot s.o./s.th./to show s.o./s.th. in extreme close-up
- to use odd/unusual camera angles
- to be filmed/shot on location/in a studio
- to be set/take place in Minnesota
- to have a happy ending/plot twist
- a shot: a single piece of film without cuts exposed continuously
- a segment: a larger unit in a film composed of a number of shots; usually the unifying elements are place, time, theme, etc.
- parallel action/cross-cutting: intermingling the shots of two or more scenes
- flashback: scene or sequence that is inserted into the "present time" and deals with the past
- flash-forward: scenes or shots referring to a future point in time
- match cut: two (or more) scenes or shots are linked by visual, aural or metaphorical parallelism
- bokeh: the blur/ the aesthetic quality of the blur in the out-of-focus areas of an image

Find more at the Movie Database online glossary: www.imdb.com/glossary

Worksheet   Working with Stills

Tasks:

Briefly describe the drawing. Sum up the scene it is taken from.
Analyse the drawing and its effect on the viewer.

Film Stills

Use appropriate cinematographic terms.
Remember: When describing, analysing and evaluating film stills, the same rules apply as for all other kinds of visual material (illustrations, photos, cartoons, pictures).

Homework Task:

Decide which scene you would like to present to the class. For example: Walt on his porch, on his birthday, after his son and his daughter-in-law have left. Take a screenshot, crop and save your movie still. While showing your still to your class, explain what one can see and which cinematographic means have been employed to purvey the meaning/message of the shot. Explain why you picked it.

One way of taking a screenshot and making a movie still:
You stop the DVD at the chosen place. Then take a screenshot, for example by pressing window sign and "print screen". Open your image editing software, e.g. *Irfanview*, and then press Ctrl + V to insert the print. Use *Irfanview* to crop your selection. Name the picture and save as "Gran Torino Walt alone", for example.
Lots of other ways are suggested, often with tutorials, when you search for "how to take a screenshot".

While/Post-viewing Activities – Gran Torino

Worksheet   Working with Hmong Actors

Tasks:

1. Discuss with your neighbour why Clint Eastwood conducted castings to find Hmong actors instead of picking Korean, Chinese or Asian-American actors.
2. Which aspects does Louisa Schein present in Extract 1?
3. How do Hmong actors feel about the film, e.g. Bee Vang (Thao), Brooke Thao (mother Lor), Kao Vang, who acts as an interpreter for her grandmother (grandma Lor). Refer to Extract 1.
4. What is Sandy Ci Moua's job? How does she see the future? (Extract 1)
5. What does Bee Vang (Thao) say about the filming three years later? State examples from Extract 2 and compare them with examples from Extract 1.
6. Find possible reasons for his change of mind.
7. Discuss if Gran Torino is a multicultural eye-opener, as participants of this event point out.

Extract 1:   Getting Hmong Right
Louisa Schein, Hmong Today, 26 Nov. 2008

Feelings run high among the actors about the coming impact of Gran Torino. Can one big-deal movie change how audiences view Hmong? "Eastwood is a miracle in the Hmong community. I hope that this really sheds some light," says Brooke Thao, "that it tells people that Hmong exist and how we helped in the war. My own father was recruited to fight for the US when he was only 14."

Asked about his impressions of the script, Bee Vang debates, "A lot of people are discussing whether this is gonna give Hmong a bad name." Online discussions buzz with questions – What about the gang image? What about the unassimilated elders? Someone suggests the film will make Hmong out to be barbarians. Others express concern that the way the ceremonial scenes were shot was inaccurate, sensationalized.

Translation is another issue. Since the screenplay was all in English, actors have to struggle to render lines in believable Hmong. And some of the lines actors ad-libbed in Hmong on camera will be tricky to translate back for subtitles. After interpreting on set for her grandma, Kao Vang affirms that "It will take someone really good."

In the end, Bee and others express confidence in their director, "Eastwood is brilliant. He should be able to do us justice."

Once Gran Torino is in theaters, the wait will be on for a film that not only tells the Hmong story, but does so from a Hmong point of view. As long-time actress, and production assistant for the Minnesota casting call, Sandy Ci Moua, puts it: "I see this as a catalyst for more Hmong to get into filmmaking." During casting Sandy was a major advocate for the hiring of Hmong actors. Now she wants something more. "Not just acting in someone else's movie, but writing, casting and producing – the things that make the story go."

(https://www.tcdailyplanet.net/hmong-actors-making-history-meet-gran-torino-family/)

Extract 2: Gran Torino Actor Reveals Behind-the-Scenes Racism

Krissy Reyes Ortiz, The Bottom Line, UCSB[3], 25 Jan. 2011

The Multicultural Center put on a program that opened the audience's eyes to the racial stereotypes portrayed in Hollywood films in addition to the unfair treatment that minority actors receive backstage. Bee Vang, actor and second-year student at Brown University, and Dr. Louisa Schein, Hmong media expert, discussed the truth of what happened behind the scenes of the movie Gran Torino.

Clint Eastwood's Gran Torino is about a racist old man named Walt who overcomes his prejudice by helping his teenager neighbour Thao. Thao is part of the Hmong community, a small ethnic Asian group.

Though many of the people who have seen the film may have gotten a sense of satisfaction and joy from seeing that Walt overcame his racism, the people who acted as the Hmong members in the movie did not. They were offended by the traces of racism that were included in the movie and that they experienced themselves on set.

Vang, who played Thao in the film, said he and the other Hmong actors were treated unfairly. Eastwood would not allow them to tweak their lines (even though he claimed that he did allow them to when asked in interviews following the release of the movie) and would not give them any tips on character building.

The actors felt degraded when they were told to "make noise" by rambling words in their language. The Hmong actors were also left out by their fellow cast members who were white. The cast members excluded them from cast events because they immediately assumed that Hmong actors were exactly like their character counterparts – unable to speak English clearly or to understand anything "American."

Vang also mentioned that he was upset by the way the Hmongs were portrayed in the film. He did not want the Hmong community – his own community – to be seen in a negative light by the audience. He pointed out that the ceremonies were not performed correctly, that some of their important political lines in the script were not subtitled into English, and that these inaccuracies led to misconceptions of the community.

UCSB first-year Jen Greenfield was surprised to hear about these truths. "When I first saw Gran Torino, I thought that it was really good because I didn't know about the whole background," she said. "This discussion has made me realize that I do approach things with a white supremacy point of view. It was interesting to hear a different perspective."
[...]
MCC associate director Viviana Marsano, who is in charge of planning the MCC's various events, was incredibly enthusiastic about providing this particular program. "The content of this workshop is exactly what the MCC is about – breaking the stereotypes of colored communities and addressing the issues of sexuality and gender. It fulfills the mission of the MCC."

(https://thebottomline.as.ucsb.edu/2011/01/gran-torino-actor-reveals-behind-the-scenes-racism)

---

[3]   UCSB = University of California, Santa Barbara

After Viewing the Film

The material suggested in this section should enable students to deal better with their exam tasks by reflecting the film and related topics.

After viewing the film students can deal with opinions and statements about **Gran Torino** and with Roger Ebert's review (page 80). They can recall their own impressions and views and add them.

As the film is set in auto city Detroit, a group work task on Detroit is included as well as some statistics for the whole class (from page 82 onwards). Students will discover that Detroit is contrary to American trends in several ways: its population comprises over 80% blacks and under 11 percent whites; over 16% have no health insurance and about 40% live in poverty.

For A-level preparations, a number of partner speaking tasks on relevant topics are included (pages 90 to 102). They deal with racism under the heading of "Neighbours"; they offer discussions on gun culture in the U.S. and refer to school shootings. "Standing your ground" and its relevance is another pair task; and also Immigration and Refugees. Additional information is included.

The topic of guilt and redemption is dealt with in a suggested class test on a veteran's trauma of war (page 103).

In a mini-project on **Identity**, students can work on "Belonging and finding (and having) one's place in society" by having a look at their own class.

The students should develop their own questions. These might help: Who speaks another language at home? Which? Which nationality/ies do your parents have? ... your grandparents?
How would you describe yourself?
Would you be a hyphenated person?
Are you proud of what you are?

In a final personal statement on page 105 a man explains the racism he encounters because he has an Asian face.

An interesting discussion can be started asking:
How do Hollywood films portray people of different races and ethnicities?
Students should be encouraged to use their own viewing experiences.

Post-viewing Activities – Gran Torino

Worksheet   Working With Reviews 1

Tasks:

Work in pairs. Rephrase your sentence. Then comment on it.

What gives the film its formidable strength is the way Eastwood shows Walt struggling with his prejudices and coming to terms with a changing world and with his inner demons, many of the latter stemming from the horrors he witnessed in the Korean War.

(Philip French, Observer (UK), Feb 26, 2009)

Eastwood is perfect as a growling cur of a man attempting to keep humanity at arm's length. Yet he's lonely, concurrently playing games of 'keep away' and 'notice me.'

(Kimberly Gadette, Indie Movies Online, Feb. 24, 2009)

This is still an enjoyably big, brash, macho melodrama, saved from absurdity by Eastwood's cracking performance.

(Peter Bradshaw, Guardian, Feb. 20, 2009)

In a way it's quite touching that Eastwood still believes a man is never too old to change. One only wishes that Gran Torino were a little more subtle and a little less earnest in its operations.

(Anthony Quinn, Independent (UK), Feb. 20, 2009)

The comedy-drama on release is actually a rather wise, insightful exploration of family and friendship, violence and vengeance.

(Geoff Andrew, Time Out, Feb. 19, 2009)

It is familiar, but only to a point. Suddenly, that point is past and much more serious questions come up, questions of responsibility, of vengeance, of the efficacy of blood for blood.

(Kenneth Turan, Los Angeles Times, Jan. 16, 2009)

Covers a lot of ground as it rolls: religion, the toll of war, mortality, what it means to be a man.

(Neil Pond, American Profile, Sept. 28, 2011)

Though the film feels like a requiem, Kowalski's heart is still defiantly beating.

(Christine Champ, film.com, May 6, 2011)

Seeing Eastwood ward off young gangsters was odd... well, but he pulled it off enough.

(Candice Frederick, Reel Talk Online, Sept. 12, 2017)

This is another Eastwood's deconstruction of his career, and it doesn't give anything else in the movie any room to breathe.

(Will Leitch, Deadspin, June 22, 2013)

Post-viewing Activities – Gran Torino

Worksheet Working With Reviews 2

Tasks:

1. Which aspect does Roger Ebert especially emphasise in his review?
2. Why might Roger Ebert have given the film only 3.5 stars out of 4?
3. Knowing the film, we see the characters clearly and understand Roger Ebert who calls Walt's grand-daughter "a self-centered greed machine". With short examples, present Ashley to someone who has not seen the film.
4. Which two main topics does Roger Ebert point out? What would you like to add?

Extract: **Gran Torino**

Roger Ebert, www.rogerebert.com, December 17, 2008

I would like to grow up to be like Clint Eastwood. Eastwood the director, Eastwood the actor. Eastwood the invincible, Eastwood the old man. What other figure in the history of the cinema has been an actor for 53 years, a director for 37, won two Oscars for direction, two more for best picture, plus the Thalberg Award, and at 78 can direct himself in his own film and look meaner than hell? None, that's how many.

"Gran Torino" stars Eastwood as an American icon once again – this time as a cantankerous, racist, beer-chugging retired Detroit autoworker who keeps his shotgun ready to lock and load. [...] Eastwood plays the character as a man bursting with energy, most of which he uses to hold himself in. Each word, each scowl, seems to have broken loose from a deep place.

Walt Kowalski calls the Asian family next door "gooks" and "chinks" and so many other names he must have made it a study. How does he think this sounds? When he gets to know Thao, the teenage Hmong who lives next door, he takes him down to his barber for a lesson in how Americans talk. He and the barber call each other a Polack and a dago and so on, and Thao is supposed to get the spirit. I found this scene far from realistic and wondered what Walt was trying to teach Thao. Then it occurred to me Walt didn't know it wasn't realistic.

Walt is not so much a racist as a security guard, protecting his own security. He sits on his porch defending the theory that your right to walk through this world ends when your toe touches his lawn. Walt's wife has just died (I would have loved to meet her), and his sons have learned once again that the old bastard wants them to stay the hell out of his business. In his eyes, they're overweight meddlers working at meaningless jobs, and his granddaughter is a self-centered greed machine.

Walt sits on his porch all day long, when he's not doing house repairs or working on his prized 1972 Gran Torino, a car he helped assemble on the Ford assembly line. He sees a lot. He sees a carload of Hmong gangstas trying to enlist the quiet, studious Thao into their thuggery. When they threaten Thao to make him try to steal the Gran Torino, Walt catches him red-handed and would just as soon shoot him as not. Then Thao's sister Sue (Ahney Her, likable and sensible) comes over to apologize for her family and offer Thao's services for odd jobs, Walt accepts only reluctantly. When Sue is threatened by some black bullies, Walt's eyes narrow and he growls and gets involved because it is his nature.

What with one thing and another, his life becomes strangely linked with these people, although Sue has to explain that the Hmong are mountain people from Laos who were U.S. allies and found it advisable to leave their homeland. When she drags him over to join a family gathering, Walt casually calls them all "gooks" and Sue a "dragon lady," they seem like awfully good sports about it, although a lot of them may not speak English. Walt seems unaware that his role is to embrace their common humanity, although he likes it when they stuff him with great-tasting Hmong food and flatter him.

Among actors of Eastwood's generation, James Garner might have been able to play this role, but my guess is, he'd be too nice in it. Eastwood doesn't play nice. Walt makes no apologies for who he is, and that's why, when he begins to decide he likes his neighbors better than his own family, it means something. "Gran Torino" isn't a liberal parable. It's more like, out of the frying pan and into the melting pot. Along the way, he fends off the sincere but very young parish priest (a persuasive Christopher Carley), who is only carrying out the deathbed wishes of the late Mrs. Kowalski. Walt is a nominal Catholic. Hardly even nominal.

"Gran Torino" is about two things, I believe. It's about the belated flowering of a man's better nature. And it's about Americans of different races growing more open to one another in the new century. This doesn't involve some kind of grand transformation. It involves starting to see the "gooks" next door as people you love. And it helps if you live in the kind of neighborhood where they are next door.

If the climax seems too generic and pre-programmed, with too much happening fairly quickly, I like that better than if it just dribbled off into sweetness. So would Walt.

3½ stars out of 4.

(https://www.rogerebert.com/reviews/gran-torino-2008)

For the teacher:

1. The person of Clint Eastwood and his acting and directing this film.
2. Probably the fast and predictable ending, although he approves of it.
3. Ashley admires Walt's vintage furniture and points out that she will go to university soon and has no furniture. Then she caresses Walt's Gran Torino and asks Walt straightaway what is going to happen to the car after his death. All through, she doesn't show any feelings towards her grandfather – during the church service she can be seen texting, she complains about there being no mobile reception at Walt's home and only very reluctantly does she offer her help with some chairs.
4. Walt is the way he is – and he undergoes a development towards more caring and understanding.

At the same time, it is about trying to understand one's neighbours; about integration; about different races living together peacefully in a multicultural society.

One could add that it is also about dealing with war trauma and about atonement for one's actions, and about finding one's place in society if we look at Thao (and at lonely Walt).

Worksheet   Detroit – Facts and Figures

Task:

With your partner, discuss the Detroit Census figures. In which categories do figures about people in Detroit widely differ from US average figures? Comment on the situation in Detroit.
(You can find more details here:
https://www.census.gov/quickfacts/fact/table/detroitcitymichigan,US/PST045217)

People	Detroit city, Michigan	United States
Population		
Population estimates July 1, 2016	672,795	323,127,513
Population estimates April 1, 2010	713,862	308,758,105
Population percent change 2010-2016	– 5.8 %	+ 4.7 %
Age and Sex (in percent)		
Persons under 5 years, April 1, 2010	7 %	6.5 %
Persons under 18 years, April 1, 2010	26.7 %	24.0 %
Persons 65 years and over, April 1, 2010	11.5 %	13.0 %
Female persons, April 1, 2010	52.7 %	50.8 %
Race and Origin (in percent)	Census 2010	figures 2016
White	10.61 %	76.9 %
Black or African American	82.62 %	13.3 %
American Indian and Alaska Native	0.37 %	1.3 %
Asian	1.06 %	5.7 %
Two or More Races	2.23 %	2.5 %
Hispanic or Latino	6.82 %	17.8 %
Population Characteristics	figures 2016	
Foreign born persons, percent, 2012-2016	5.5 %	13.2 %
Housing		
Housing units 2010	349,170	131,704,730
Owner-occupied housing unit rate, 2012-2016	48.2 %	63.6 %
Median value of owner-occupied housing units, 2010-2016	$ 41,000	$ 184,700
Median gross rent, 2012-2016	$ 754	$ 949
Families and Living Arrangements 2012-2016		
Households	256,985	117,716,237
Persons per household	2.61	2.64
Language other than English spoken at home, percent of persons age 5+	10.5 %	21.1 %

Education (in percent), 2012-2016		
High school graduate or higher, age 25+	79.0 %	87.0 %
Bachelor's degree or higher, age 25+	13.8 %	30.3 %
Health (in percent)		
With a disability, under age 65, 2012-2016	16.3 %	8.6 %
Persons without health insurance, under age 65	▲ 16.4 %	▲ 10.1 %
Economy (2012-2016)		
In civilian labor force, total, age 16+, percent	53.5 %	63.1 %
Total retail sales per capita, 2012	$ 4,557	$ 13,443
Income and Poverty		
Median household income, 2012-2016	$ 26,249	$ 55,322
Per capita income in past 12 months, 2012-2016	$ 15,562	$ 29,829
Persons in poverty, percent	▲ 39.4 %	▲ 12.7 %

For the teacher:

The fact that in Detroit about 11% whites face about 82% blacks will astonish students, as it is more or less the opposite of US figures. By the way, in Michigan, the overall figure of blacks is only 13 percent. In Detroit, there are fewer owner-owned homes; there is visible and blatant poverty (nearly 40%); one sixth of the population is without health insurance; there is a much higher rate of people with disabilities. The ▲ sign is used in the official statistics to point out some of these note-worthy facts.
There are far fewer foreign born people in Detroit, and far fewer Latinos than average.
Detroit is losing inhabitants, while on average, the US is gaining inhabitants.
We remember the fact that in 2013, Detroit went bankrupt.

Detroit remains one of the most racially segregated cities in the US. In 1910 fewer than 6,000 blacks lived here, but in 1930 the figure had already risen to more than 120,000. Many more arrived from the 1940s to the 1970s to escape Jim Crow laws and discrimination in the south and to find jobs in the motor industry (= Great Migration).
In the first decade of the 21st century, about two-thirds of the total black population in Detroit's metropolitan area resided within the city limits of Detroit.

As of 2006, the city has one of the largest concentrations of Hmong Americans. About 4,000 Hmong and other Asian immigrant families live in Detroit. Hmong immigrant families generally have lower incomes than other Asian families, and bigger families (5.8 persons).

Find out more about Hmong Americans here:
https://cdn.americanprogress.org/wp-content/uploads/2015/04/AAPI-Hmong-factsheet.pdf

Post-viewing Activities and Exam Preparation

Worksheet   Detroit and the American Dream (Group Work)

Task:

Do the tasks given to your group. Then present the results and fill in the overview table.

	Short Title	Brief Summary
1	Growing Up Hmong in Detroit	
2	In Detroit, the End of Blight is in Sight	
3	Want the most American car or truck?	
4	Believe in America	
5	Now and Then	

For the teacher: The filled-in table should include the following:

	Short Title	Brief Summary
1	Growing Up Hmong in Detroit	At the University of Michigan two female Hmong students present the problems Hmong have at school: high dropout-rates, precarious living conditions, traditional obligations towards their family, and parents who speak only little English. – All these problems can be found in Gran Torino.
2	In Detroit, the End of Blight is in Sight	Detroit is recovering after the end of the bankruptcy proceedings in 2014, when its new mayor took office. Among other things, he has greatly improved the response time for ambulances and police; he is now tackling the demolition of empty, falling-down buildings. By getting the city to the "right size" (=smaller), road repair, etc., will be affordable. – We see derelict areas and abandoned places where the gangs cruise.
3	Want the most American car or truck?	Although the car industry is becoming more global, three General Motors models head the list if you want to "buy American"; next is a Ford pick-up truck. Over 7 million people work in the car industry. The 17.5 million vehicles sold comprise 3.5% of the U.S. gross domestic product. – Since Walt worked for the Ford company all his life, it matters to him.
4	Believe in America	The American Dream can come true because car companies are expanding in the U.S. and are building new production plants; and work places are moving (back) to America. – Perhaps they might not only want work places but clean nature? Better schools? Less guns?
5	Now and Then	In this interview Clint Eastwood comes across as an outspoken, old-fashioned man with traditional values: people should get going and work to achieve their aims. He complains about the "pussy generation" today. – Add a few racist slurs, and you have Walt Kowalski.

Post-viewing Activities and Exam Preparation

Worksheet   Detroit and the Hmong – Group 1

Task:

Summarise the text.
Refer to the Hmong characters in Gran Torino and point out common points and differences.

Extract: **Growing Up Hmong in Detroit**
Kimberley Chou, The Michigan Daily, 7 December 2006

Asian Americans make up one of the best-represented minority groups at Ann Arbor, home of the University of Michigan. But their path to university isn't always easy – especially if it starts in Detroit.

● Maichou Lor and Dia Shia Yang, both high school seniors of Hmong heritage, and history Prof. Scott Kurashige underscored this point.

Students at Detroit's Osborn High School, Lor and Yang spoke about the difficulties of being Hmong in Detroit. They said their traditional familial obligations and immigrant parents who speak little English often make their high school careers different from the typical American experience.

The Hmong are one of largest ethnic minority groups in Southeast Asia. Many Hmong fled from Laos to the United States during the Vietnam War and the Laotian conflict. In the United States, Hmong are among the least affluent Asian immigrant groups. Detroit is home to one of the largest concentrations of Hmong in the United States.

Lor and Yang described what it is like to attend a high school often criticized for its lack of resources and tension among students. Dropouts, too, are common. When Lor started at Osborn in 2003, there were about 700 students in her class. Now there are 200.

Lor and Yang both participate in the Detroit Asian Youth Project, a student-founded group based in Detroit. The group's mission is to help Asian American teenagers in Detroit learn about Asian cultures, ● develop leadership skills and promote social and political self-awareness. The DAY Project mostly works with Hmong youth as Hmong make up the majority of Detroit's Asian community.

"It really helps us in learning about society," said Lor, who said she works two jobs outside of school to support her family. "It inspires us to be college students." She said she plans to attend college. "Wherever I go – Detroit is my hometown," she said. "I'm definitely coming back to Detroit."

That's exactly the attitude the DAY Project advocates. On its xanga.com homepage, the group lists "Detroit revitalization" and "Chinatown revitalization" among its interests.
(https://www.michigandaily.com/content/growing-hmong-detroit)

* * *

In order to find out more about the DAY project in Detroit, go to
http://www.uixdetroit.com/projects/dayproject.aspx and
https://www.nbcnews.com/news/asian-america/detroit-asian-youth-project-celebrates-10-years-mentorship-n186796

Post-viewing Activities and Exam Preparation

Worksheet   Detroit – Fixing the City – Group 2

Task:

Summarise this extract. Point out which aspects of Detroit Walt Kowalski can confirm.

Extract: In Detroit, the End of Blight is in Sight
Economist, 16 September 2017

The once-great city, the "arsenal of democracy" during the Second World War and home of the world's most innovative manufacturers, has almost been ruined [...]. National interest in Detroit has waned since its bankruptcy proceedings, brought on by decades of mismanagement, ended in December 2014. Most tales of the city now take one of two tacks. Either Detroit remains mired in poverty and unemployment, its doom merely forestalled by a few years. Or the hipsters flooding in are, with each overwrought coffee contraption and jam-jar cocktail, returning the city to something like its former glory.

What both accounts miss is that Detroit seems on the point of doing something remarkable: re-electing a mayor whose singular achievement has been to knock bits of the city down faster than his predecessors. Mike Duggan took office in 2014. He is the city's first white mayor in 40 years. In the past four decades the city has undergone a racial transformation: from 70% white in the 1960s to just 10% now.

The mayor's meeting room is blanketed in graphs charting the city's employment, ambulance delivery and crime rates, among other statistics. "The police are going to show up in under 14 minutes; the ambulance is going to show up in under 8 minutes; the grass is going to be cut in the parks every 10 to 12 days – it just is." Employees who do not meet these targets do not last long.

Plenty of these numbers have improved. Police response times are down from an average of 40 minutes to 13. But the most important numbers for Detroit's future concern derelict properties. There were 40,000 such structures in 2014 – ruins left over from an extreme population crunch. The sprawling metropolis, covering 139 square miles, once housed 1.8m people – three times as many as today. Urbanists suggest that the solution for such cities is "right-sizing" – shrinking them down to a size where the city can afford to provide pavements, streetlights, sewerage and so on.

Wholesale restructuring of Detroit inspires scepticism, because past city efforts hurt black residents in the name of development. Albert Cobo, mayor for much of the 1950s, pursued the building of motorways by razing black neighbourhoods, sowing the seeds for the race riots in 1967 which marked, for many, the beginning of Detroit's decline.

That means the task has to be accomplished by persuasion instead. Since Mr Duggan took office, the city has demolished 11,900 residential properties. The demolition of a blighted property increases the value of a home 500 feet away by 4.2%, according to a study. The pace has been unprecedented.

(https://www.economist.com/news/united-states/21728959-what-happens-when-city-accustomed-bad-government-elects-good-one-detroit-end)

Worksheet   Detroit – Buying American – Group 3

Task:

Summarise this extract.
Point out why "buying American" matters to Walt Kowalski. Also mention his attitude towards those who don't buy American.

Extract: Want the most American car or truck? Here are the models.
Sophia Tulp, USA TODAY, 18 July 2017

If "Buying American" matters to you, Detroit offers some cars and truck models with the most U.S. parts and labor, even as the industry becomes ever-more global.

Three General Motors models – Buick Enclave, GMC Acadia and Chevrolet Traverse – were tied at the top of the list of the most American-made car models in the 2017 Kogod Made in America Auto Index, as compiled by the business school at American University.

Next came Ford's F-150 pickup truck, followed by another GM model, the Chevrolet Corvette.

The index works by taking into account several factors that go into the assembly of a car. This includes the percentage of U.S. or Canadian parts used, the location of the factory where the vehicle was assembled, the source of the engine and transmission and whether more than 15% of the parts came from a foreign country. Each category receives its own score.

Over the past five years since the index began, overall American content and labor in cars has been decreasing, finds Frank DuBois, a professor at American University's Kogod School of Business. It's down about five percentage points.

In tying for first place, the Enclave, Acadia and Traverse all received a score of 85.5.

The results were celebrated by a lobbying organization for Detroit's Big 3 – GM, Ford and Fiat-Chrysler.

"America's three auto manufacturers once again dominated," said Matt Blunt, president of the American Automotive Policy Council.

In 2016, the auto industry supplied over 7 million jobs and sold 17.5 million vehicles. They comprised 3.5% of the nation's gross domestic product. Some 65% of those vehicles were produced in the U.S., a slight increase over 2015 sales which broke a 15-year record, according to the Alliance of Automobile Manufacturers.

(https://www.usatoday.com/story/money/cars/2017/06/08/study-finds-detroit-still-rules-american-made-cars/102651126/)

Post-viewing Activities and Exam Preparation

Worksheet   American Dream – Group 4

Task:

Discuss this extract from President Trump's State of the Union Address (Jan 2018).
Relate it to the characters of Walt, of Thao and of Sue in *Gran Torino*. Point out what they might agree with and what not.

Extract: **Believe in America**
President Donald Trump, State of the Union Address, 30 January 2018

This, in fact, is our new American moment. There has never been a better time to start living the American dream. So, to every citizen watching at home tonight, no matter where you have been or where you have come from, this is your time. If you work hard, if you believe in yourself, if you believe in America, then you can dream anything, be anything. And together, we can achieve absolutely anything. (Applause)

Tonight, I want to talk about what kind of future we are going to have, and what kind of a nation we are going to be. All of us, together, as one team, one people, and one American family, can do anything. We all share the same home, the same heart, the same destiny, and the same great American flag.

In our drive to make Washington accountable, we have eliminated more regulations in our first year than any administration in the history of our country. (Applause)

We have ended the war on American energy, and we have ended the war on beautiful clean coal. (Applause) We are now very proudly an exporter of energy to the world. (Applause)

In Detroit, I halted government mandates that crippled America's great, beautiful autoworkers so that we can get Motor City revving its engines again. And that's what's happening. (Applause) Many car companies are now building and expanding plants in the United States – something we haven't seen for decades. Chrysler is moving a major plant from Mexico to Michigan. Toyota and Mazda are opening up a plant in Alabama – a big one. And we haven't seen this in a long time. It's all coming back. (Applause)

Very soon, auto plants and other plants will be opening up all over our country. This is all news Americans are totally unaccustomed to hearing. For many years, companies and jobs were only leaving us. But now they are roaring back. They're coming back. They want to be where the action is. They want to be in the United States of America. That's where they want to be. (Applause)

(https://www.whitehouse.gov/briefings-statements/remarks-president-trump-state-union-address/)

Post-viewing Activities and Exam Preparation

Worksheet   American Dream – Group 5

Task:

From this extract from the interview Clint Eastwood and his son gave to Esquire in 2016, point out some of Clint Eastwood's character traits.
Which of them does he also portray in **Gran Torino**?

Extract: **Now and Then**
Clint Eastwood/Michael Hainey, Interview with Esquire, Aug. 3, 2016

CE: We're really in a pussy generation. Everybody's walking on eggshells. We see people accusing people of being racist and all kinds of stuff. When I grew up, those things weren't called racist. And then when I did **Gran Torino**, even my associate said, "This is a really good script, but it's politically incorrect." And I said, "Good. Let me read it tonight." The next morning, I came in and threw it on his desk and I said, "We're starting this immediately."

ESQ: What is the "pussy generation"?

CE: All these people that say "Oh, you can't do that, and you can't do this, and you can't say that." I guess it's just the times.
[...]
CE: When I harken back to my dad, I remember we left Redding and drove down here so he could get a job as a gas jockey at a Standard Station on the corner of PCH and Sunset Boulevard. But you travel five hundred miles, bring your family, rip up everything, and do that because that's the only job that existed. So I think, *What would happen if he'd have said, "Oh, I can't do that?"* Well, we'd have been begging for sandwiches at somebody's backdoor. Which is, I remember, one of the most affecting things that ever happened in my life. I was a little kid, five years old, and a guy comes to the back of our house and says to my mother, "There's a bunch of wood in the back. Could I chop that up for you, ma'am?" And my mother says, "We don't have money." And he says, "I don't want any money. Just a sandwich."

[Clint goes silent; his eyes well up.]

ESQ: Does that memory haunt you?

CE: It haunts me when I think of all the assholes out there who are complaining. I saw people who really had it bad. There was no welfare to catch, to fill the bill there. The guy just wanted a sandwich. Hopefully later on he got a job somewhere. He was a guy trying to exist, and that's the way people were then.

(You can find the full interview here:
https://www.esquire.com/entertainment/a46893/double-trouble-clint-and-scott-eastwood/)

Post-viewing Activities – Speaking Tasks

Worksheet   Neighbours/Living Together – Partner 1

Tasks:

1. Briefly describe the extract from a flyer which was distributed in Montgomery County in January 2018. Analyse its contents. Talk about possible reactions in the neighbourhood. (5 minutes)

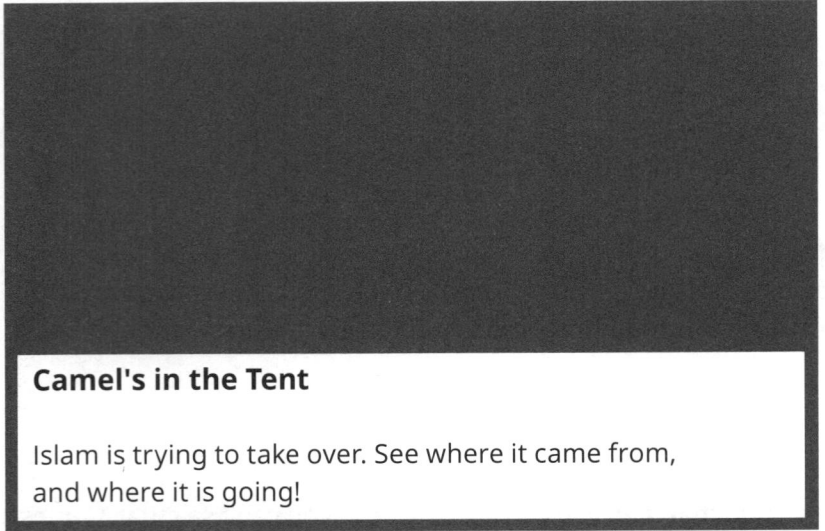

Camel's in the Tent

Islam is trying to take over. See where it came from, and where it is going!

This is their pattern for conquest:

Infiltrate ...   (Move in)

Populate ...   (Grow large families and recruit others)

Legislate ...   (Make laws against converting Muslims)

Decimate ...   (Take over the country little by little, one city at a time)

Eliminate ...   (Destroy those who do not submit to Sharia law)

America's next!
(Find more at: http://www.chick.com/reading/tracts/1081/1081_01.asp)

2. With your partner, discuss this quote by Martin Luther King and relate it to events in the US.

"The ultimate measure of a man is not where he stands in moments of comfort and convenience, but where he stands in times of challenge and controversy. The true neighbor will risk his position, his prestige, and even his life for the welfare of others." (*Strength to Love, 1963*) (10 minutes)

Post-viewing Activities – Speaking Tasks

Worksheet   Neighbours/Living Together – Partner 2

Tasks:

1. Briefly describe the sign in front of a church in Harrisonburg, Virginia.
   Analyse its contents. Talk about possible reactions in the neighbourhood. (5 minutes)

(Sign put up in front of the Immanuel Mennonite Church in Harrisonburg, VA, in 2015)

2. With your partner, discuss this quote by Martin Luther King and relate it to events in the US.

"The ultimate measure of a man is not where he stands in moments of comfort and convenience, but where he stands in times of challenge and controversy. The true neighbor will risk his position, his prestige, and even his life for the welfare of others." (*Strength to Love, 1963*)   (10 minutes)

Post-viewing Activities – Speaking Tasks

Worksheet   Gun Control – Partner 1

Tasks:

1. Summarize the opinions stated by these two women after the mass shooting in Parkland, Florida, which killed 17 students on Feb 14, 2018. Present your ideas on the topic. (5 minutes)

Tomi Lahren@TomiLahren via Twitter.
Can the Left let the families grieve for even 24 hours before they push their anti-gun and anti-gunowner agenda? My goodness. This isn't about a gun it's about another lunatic.
#FloridaShooting   4:29PM – Feb 15, 2018

Jennifer Baker; NRA spokeswoman:
"We need serious proposals to prevent violent criminals and the dangerously mentally ill from acquiring firearms." "Legislative proposals that prevent law-abiding adults aged 18-20 years from acquiring rifles and shotguns effectively prohibits them for purchasing any firearm, thus depriving them of their constitutional right to self-protection." (Feb. 21, 2018)

2. With your partner, discuss this tweet by President Donald Trump after his meeting with Parkland students; and its future repercussions. (10 minutes)

"History shows that a school shooting last[sic], on average, 3 minutes. It takes police & first responders approximately 5 to 8 minutes to get to site of crime. Highly trained, gun adept, teachers/coaches would solve the problem instantly, before police arrive. GREAT DETERRENT! (1:54 PM – Feb 22, 2018)

For the teacher:

Additional material:

Donald J. Trump ✔  Follow
@realDonaldTrump

What many people don't understand, or don't want to understand, is that Wayne, Chris and the folks who work so hard at the @NRA are Great People and Great American Patriots. They love our Country and will do the right thing!   MAKE AMERICA GREAT AGAIN!

3:31 PM - Feb 22, 2018

♥ 86.3K   💬 64.8K people are talking about this

Worksheet   Gun Control – Partner 2

Tasks:

1. Summarize the opinion of these men after the mass shooting in Parkland, Florida, which killed 17 students on Feb 14. Present your views on the topic. (5 minutes)

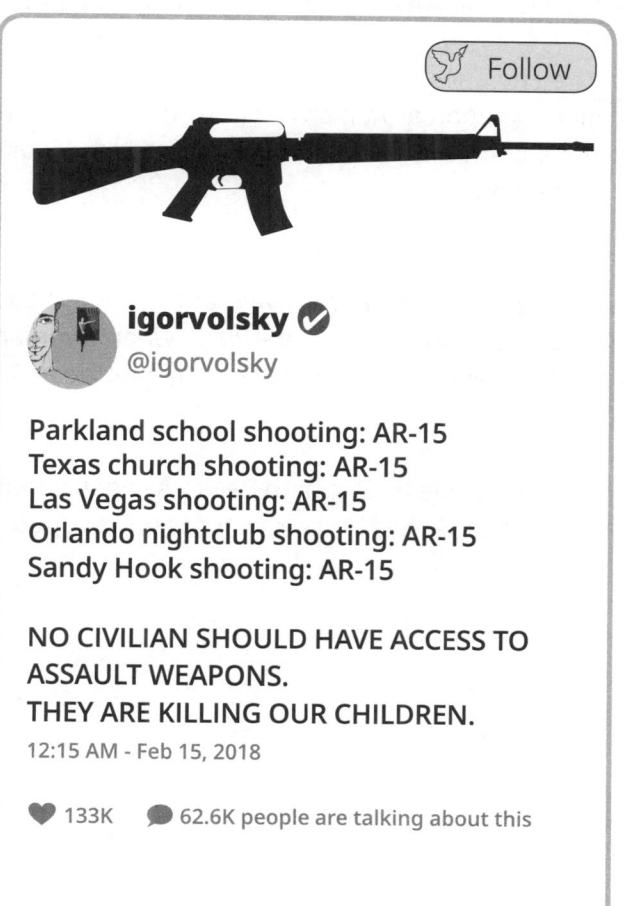

Follow

igorvolsky ✓
@igorvolsky

Parkland school shooting: AR-15
Texas church shooting: AR-15
Las Vegas shooting: AR-15
Orlando nightclub shooting: AR-15
Sandy Hook shooting: AR-15

NO CIVILIAN SHOULD HAVE ACCESS TO
ASSAULT WEAPONS.
THEY ARE KILLING OUR CHILDREN.

12:15 AM - Feb 15, 2018

♥ 133K   💬 62.6K people are talking about this

Follow

Jeff Flake ✓
@JeffFlake

A kid too young to buy a handgun should be too young to buy an #AR-15. Working with @SenFeinstein on a bipartisan bill that will raise the minimum purchase age for non-military buyers from 18 to 21 - the same age you currently have to be to purchase a handgun.

6:39 PM - Feb 21, 2018

♥ 23.3K   💬 7,437 people are talking about this

2. In a discussion with your partner, present this opinion stated by Patricia Arquette on Feb 14, 2018. "If people can blame drug dealers for the drug problem then we can blame the NRA for the mass shooting problem."
Add your own reflections. (10 minutes)

Post-viewing Activities – Speaking Tasks

Worksheet   Gun Control/Changes – Partner 1

Tasks:

1. Sum up what Samuel Zeif states. Add your own reflections. (5 minutes)
   Samuel Zeif, 18, is one of the students present at the school shooting in Parkland, Florida, in Feb. 2018 who give their views to President Donald Trump. He dissolves into tears as he begs the president:
   "Let's never let this happen again – please, please." Then he goes on:
   "I don't understand why I can still go in a store and buy a weapon of war, an A-R (=AR-15 rifle). How is it that easy to buy this type of weapon? How do we not stop this after Columbine, after Sandy Hook? I'm sitting with a mother who lost her son. It's still happening."

2. Since 2013, there have been 291 reported school shootings in America, which averages to about one a week. The latest shooting in Florida is thought to be one of the worst since 2012, when gunman Adam Lanza attacked Sandy Hook Elementary School in Newtown, Connecticut. He shot dead 20 young children and six adults before killing himself.

Discuss with your partner if appeals to a change of policy (like the one by Elizabeth Banks; see below) will be successful regarding the power of the National Rifle Association (the NRA) – which has huge support across much of the country. (10 minutes)

Follow

Elizabeth Banks ✔
@ElizabethBanks

Sending my love to #parkland. #guncontrol #policyandchange
1:51 AM - Feb 15, 2018

♥ 19.9K   💬 6,780 people are talking about this

Post-viewing Activities – Speaking Tasks

Worksheet   Gun Control/Changes – Partner 2

Tasks:

1. Present Kim Kardashian's statement and your own opinion as to the school shooting in Florida in Feb. 2018, which left 17 students dead. (5 minutes)

2. Since 2013, there have been 291 reported school shootings in America, which averages to about one a week. The latest shooting in Florida is thought to be one of the worst since 2012, when gunman Adam Lanza attacked Sandy Hook Elementary School in Newtown, Connecticut. He shot dead 20 young children and six adults before killing himself.

Discuss with your partner if appeals to a change of policy (like the one by Elizabeth Banks; see below) will be successful regarding the power of the National Rifle Association (the NRA) – which has huge support across much of the country. (10 minutes)

Kim Kardashian West
@KimKardashian

We owe it to our children and our teachers to keep them safe while at school. Prayers won't do this: action will, Congress, please do your job and protect Americans from senseless gun violence.

1:22 AM - Feb 15, 2018

461K   104K people are talking about this

Elizabeth Banks ✓
@ElizabethBanks

Sending my love to #parkland. #guncontrol #policyandchange

1:51 AM - Feb 15, 2018

19.9K   6,780 people are talking about this

Extract 1: A Mass Shooting in Texas and False Arguments Against Gun Control

Adam Gopnik, The New Yorker, 6 November, 2017

Twenty-six dead and twenty wounded. In a church, too, small children ripped apart. Who did it? A man with a history of domestic abuse, wearing a ballistic vest, and using an assault-type rifle. Yes, that's real enough. That one counts as a massacre.

[...]

Feelings of powerlessness and depression are bound to infect those – by all surveys, the majority of Americans – who would like to see something done to prevent these increasingly common occurrences of mass slaughter. It's hard to be hopeful. If nothing was done after the killing of twenty school children and six adults in Newtown, Connecticut, and if nothing was done – not even the "bump stock" limitation – after the murder of fifty-eight concertgoers from a sniper's perch in Las Vegas, a month ago, then twenty-six more dead won't alter things. But there is never a time to give way to hopelessness: the politics are hard but far from insurmountable, and meanwhile, as with every public crisis, the truth matters and clarifies and brings light, even when the light can't immediately show a better path forward. If we can't defeat the gun lobby now, we can out-argue it, and expose it.

(https://www.newyorker.com/news/daily-comment/a-mass-shooting-in-texas-and-false-arguments-against-gun-control)

Extract 2: Parents and Students Plead with Trump

Julie Hirschfeld Davies, The New York Times, 21 Feb. 2018

Mark Barden, who lost his 7-year-old son Daniel at Sandy Hook Elementary School in Newtown, Conn., in 2012, said it was futile to believe Congress would act on new policies. "We tried this legislative approach," said Mr. Barden, a founder and managing director of Sandy Hook Promise, a non-profit advocacy group created after the massacre. "I've been in this building before many times, wringing our hands, pleading with legislators – 'What can we do?' – until we finally said we have to go home and do this ourselves."

He and Nicole Hockley, who lost her 6-year-old son Dylan at Sandy Hook, pressed Mr. Trump to consider prevention programs that train schools and educators to identify students in crisis and intervene before they attempt to harm themselves or others. "Rather than arm them with a firearm," Ms. Hockley said of teachers, "I would rather arm them with the knowledge of how to prevent these acts from happening in the first place."

(https://www.nytimes.com/2018/02/21/us/politics/trump-guns-school-shooting.html)

Extract 3: Compton School Police Cleared to Carry AR-15 Rifles in Cars

Miriam Hernandez, KABC, 14 August 2014

High-powered rifles in the hands of Compton School Police: Do they protect students, or are they a danger to them? Compton officials defend their new policy.

(http://abc7.com/news/compton-school-police-to-carry-ar-15-rifles-in-cars/269937)

4. Check out the **NRA's 24-hour TV** at www.NRATV.com

Post-viewing Activities – Speaking Tasks

Worksheet   Stand your Ground – Partner 1

Tasks:

1. In 2012, self-appointed neighbourhood watchman George Zimmermann shot unarmed 17-year-old black Trayvon Martin in a gated community in Sanford, Florida. Zimmermann was acquitted of second-degree murder and manslaughter charges in 2013, according to existing stand-your-ground laws.
   Present the "Stand your ground" principle, its background and its relevance today. (5 minutes)

2. With your partner, discuss the statement that homicide rates have risen because of changed stand-your-ground and self-defence rights. (10 minutes)
   Take this graph into consideration and present your own opinion.

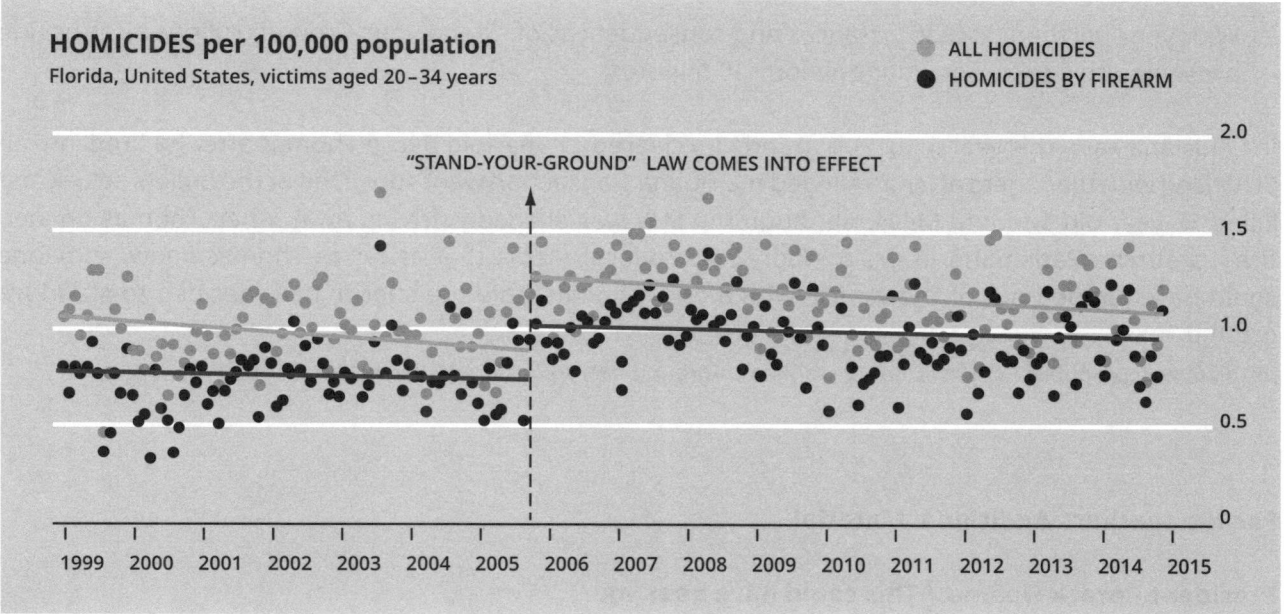

(The Economist, 7 Jan. 2017)

Post-viewing Activities – Speaking Tasks

Worksheet   Stand your Ground – Partner 2

Tasks:

1. Present these gun-carrying men and their fears. Add your opinion. (5 minutes)

Everywhere he goes on his cattle ranch, Jim Chilton has a gun at the ready. He has guns at his front door, guns in his pickup truck, guns on his horse's saddle. His fear? Coming across a bandit or a smuggler on his land northwest of Nogales, Arizona. [...] Cattleman and veterinarian Gary Thrasher frequently encounters immigrants and smugglers running through his property. Some have showered in his barn. He and his family live in constant dread.

(https://www.usatoday.com/story/news/nation/2013/02/23/what-does-a-secure-border-look-like/1941333/)

2. With your partner, discuss instances and consequences of "Stand your Ground" rulings after having presented this case. Add your opinion. (10 minutes)

In Louisiana early this year (=2012), a grand jury cleared 21-year-old Byron Thomas after he fired into an SUV filled with teenagers after an alleged marijuana transaction went sour. One of the bullets struck and killed 15-year-old Jamonta Miles. Although the SUV was allegedly driving away when Thomas opened fire, Lafourche Parish Sheriff Craig Webre said to local media that as far as Thomas knew, someone could have jumped out of the vehicle with a gun. Thomas, said the sheriff, had "decided to stand his ground."

(https://www.propublica.org/article/five-stand-your-ground-cases-you-should-know-about)

For the teacher: Additional Material

President Barack Obama: "This could have been me."

On July 19th, 2013, after the acquittal of self-appointed neighbourhood watchman George Zimmermann for shooting unarmed Trayvon Martin, President Barack Obama makes the following statements in a speech.
"You know, when Trayvon Martin was shot, I said that this could have been my son. Another way of saying that is Trayvon Martin could have been me 35 years ago.
There are very few African-American men in this country who haven't had the experience of being followed when they were shopping in a department store. That includes me. [...]
There are very few African-Americans who haven't had the experience of getting on an elevator and a woman clutching her purse nervously and holding her breath until she had a chance to get off. [...]
The African-American community is also knowledgeable that there is a history of racial disparities in the application of our criminal laws, everything from the death penalty to enforcement of our drug laws. And that ends up having an impact in terms of how people interpret the case. [...]"

Post-viewing Activities – Speaking Tasks

Worksheet   Immigration/Refugees/American Dream – Partner 1

Tasks:

1. Briefly present this poster. Add your opinion on the DREAM Act. (5 minutes)

2. What obligation, if any, do nations have towards refugees and illegal immigrants? Discuss with regard to these figures and graphs from 2018. (10 minutes)

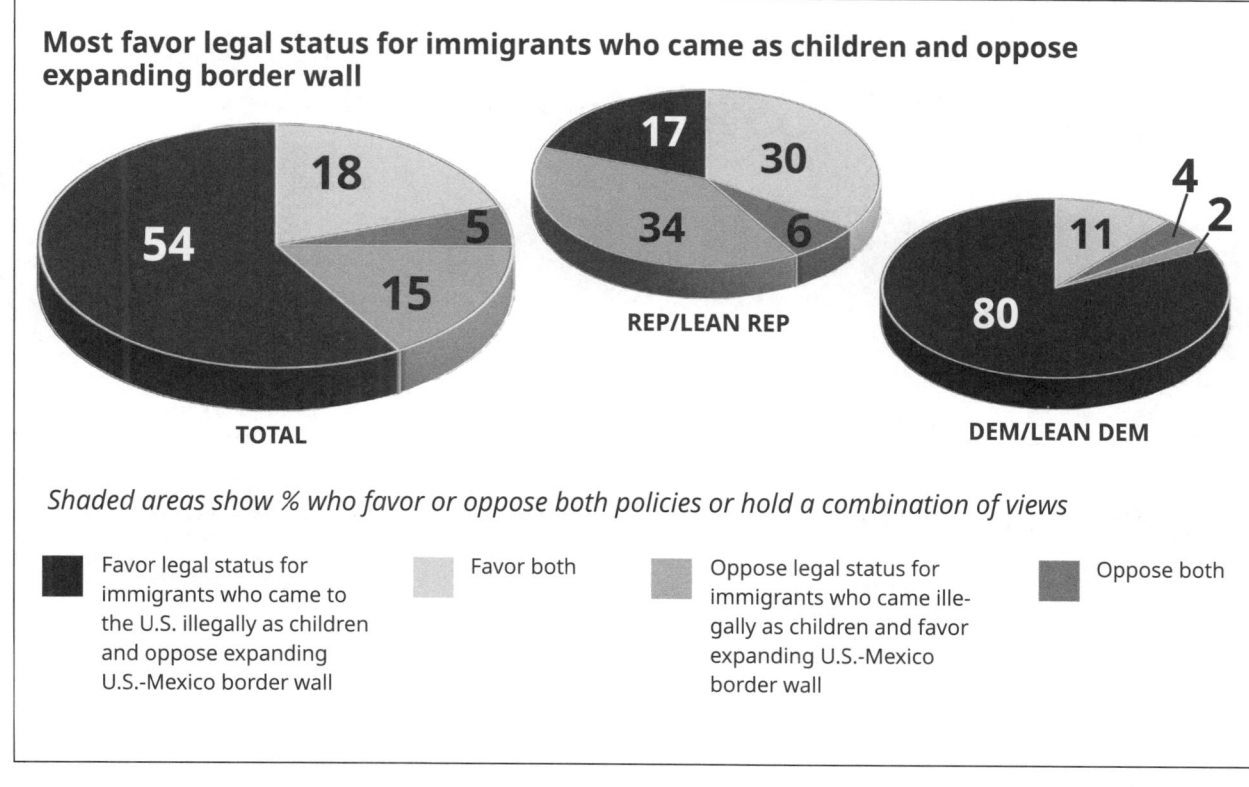

Most favor legal status for immigrants who came as children and oppose expanding border wall

TOTAL

REP/LEAN REP

DEM/LEAN DEM

Shaded areas show % who favor or oppose both policies or hold a combination of views

- Favor legal status for immigrants who came to the U.S. illegally as children and oppose expanding U.S.-Mexico border wall
- Favor both
- Oppose legal status for immigrants who came illegally as children and favor expanding U.S.-Mexico border wall
- Oppose both

Post-viewing Activities – Speaking Tasks

Worksheet Immigration/Refugees/American Dream – Partner 2

Tasks:

1. Briefly summarize the facts and comment on them. Include your views. (5 minutes)

The United States has declared the violence against Rohingya Muslims in Burma to be "ethnic cleansing", putting more pressure on the country's military to halt a crackdown that has sent more than 600,000 refugees flooding over the border to Bangladesh. Although the military has blamed Rohingya insurgents for setting off the crisis, US Secretary of State Rex Tillerson said that "no provocation can justify the horrendous atrocities that have ensued." (Nov. 2017)

2. What obligation, if any, do nations have towards refugees and illegal immigrants? Discuss with regard to these figures, statistics, graphs. (10 minutes)

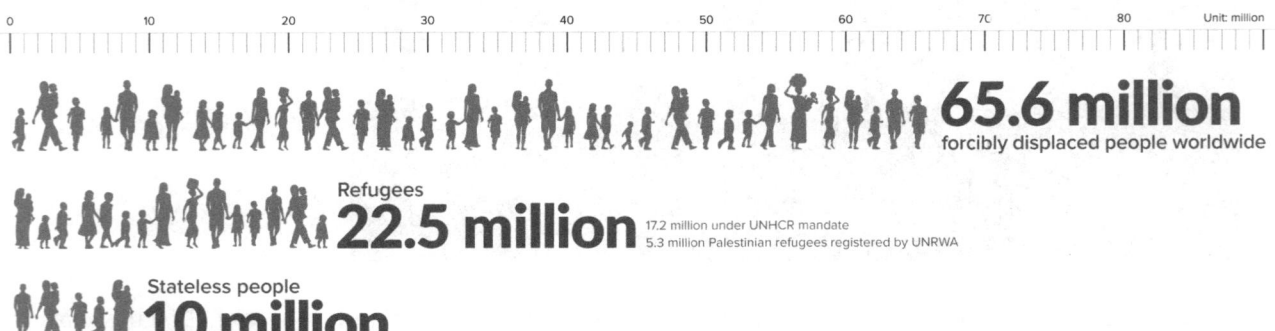

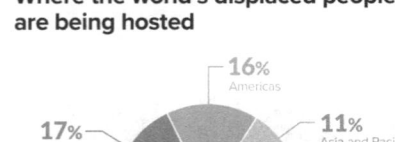

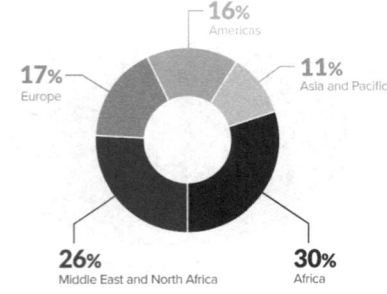

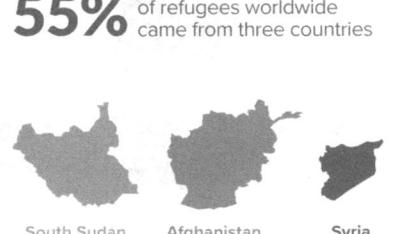

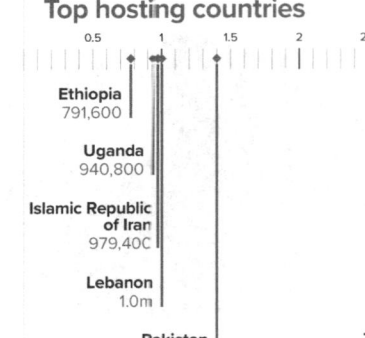

28,300 people
a day **forced to flee** their homes
because of conflict and persecution

10,966 staff
UNHCR employs 10,966 staff
(as of 30 June 2017)

130 countries
We work in 130 countries
(as of 30 June 2017)

We are funded almost entirely by voluntary contributions, with 87 per cent from governments and the European Union.

http://www.unhcr.org/figures-at-a-glance.html   (2016 figures)

Source: UNHCR / 19 June 2017

For the teacher: Additional Material

1. The AALDEF: An Asian American Democracy Project

AALDEF believes in immigration policy that adheres to basic human rights principles. This belief reso-nates throughout our work in this program area. AALDEF is an active voice on immigration policy and immigrant rights issues on a national level and is also among the few groups that provide both direct legal representation and community education to Asian immigrants and their families.

Since 1974, AALDEF has represented Asian immigrant families and workers of all backgrounds. We believe that U.S. immigration laws must close the ever-widening gap in substantive and procedural rights between immigrant Americans and U.S.-born Americans, respect the rights of all workers, and maintain family reunification as a core value. In 2006, AALDEF was involved in efforts calling for the reform of national immigration policy, but legislative efforts ultimately failed. Today, we urge members of Congress to adhere to human rights principles in guiding the current debate on comprehensive immigration reform.
(http://aaldef.org)

- *Why We Rise* is a compelling short documentary featuring three brave young Asian New Yorkers who reveal what it's like to grow up without having legal immigration status. Their struggles and their strength are on full display as they come out of the shadows and into the light.

"I can't get a job. I can't start a career."
"I can't totally relax. I have to be careful of what to say, and what not to say."
"I can't have my parents by my side."
"I can't sleep at night, because I'm worried about immigration agents breaking down my door."

Why We Rise was filmed by Brian Redondo and Corinne Manabat with the support of the Asian American Legal Defense and Education Fund. It premiered May 20, 2013 in front of a packed audience at #Undoc-uAsians, a theatre performance by RAISE at The Culture Project.

You can contact RAISE members at info@aaldef.org
You can find further information at http://aaldef.org/raise.html

You can find the short documentary at https://www.youtube.com/watch?time_continue048&v= u5va8nVRi0o

-

2. From Dishwasher to Heart Doctor; Atlanta Refugee Embodies American Story

In this short video (2:32 minutes) from 18 February, 2018, Dr. Heval Mohamed Kelli is presented who started his American experience as a 14-year-old refugee from Syria. He is now a cardiologist at Emory University Hospital in Atlanta. On Sundays he regularly helps out in the community's medical centre and treats immigrants, who – like his family when they arrived – have no health coverage.
Find the video here:
https://www.voanews.com/a/dishwasher-to-heart-doctor-atlanta-refugee-embodies-american-story/4259121.html

3. From Refugee to Mayor: First Vietnamese-American Elected Mayor of Little Saigon

Tri Ta was born in Saigon, Vietnam and came to the United States as a political refugee when he was 19 years old. Now he is Mayor of Westminster, California.
Find the story and 4-minute video here, published on Feb. 28, 2018:
https://www.voanews.com/a/tri-ta-vietnamese-mayor-little-siagon/4274848.html

4. Temporary Protected Status

More than 320,000 immigrants from 10 nations have permission to live and work in the U.S. under Temporary Protected Status (TPS), because war, hurricanes or other disasters in their home countries could make it dangerous for them to return. Many are expected to lose their benefits in 2018 and 2019. The Trump administration has said it will not renew the program for people from El Salvador, Haiti, Nicaragua and Sudan, who together account for about 76% of enrolled immigrants.

Task:

From the table, point out when the various groups will lose their benefits.

Immigrants from 10 nations have Temporary Protected Status		
NATION	ESTIMATE	EXPIRES
Nepal	8,950	JUNE 24, 2018
Honduras	57,000	July 5, 2018
Yemen	1,000	Sept. 3, 2018
Somalia	250	Sept. 17, 2018
Sudan	1,040	Nov. 2, 2018
Nicaragua	2,550	Jan. 5, 2019
South Sudan	70	May 2, 2019
Haiti	46,000	July 22, 2019
El Salvador	195,000	Sept. 9, 2019
Syria	7,000	Sept. 30, 2019

▨ Trump administration says it will not renew*

* Administration positions as of Feb. 22, 2018.
Note: For Syrians, TPS only available for those who have been in the U.S. since Aug. 1, 2016.
Source: U.S. Department of Homeland Security estimates included in Federal Register notices, 2016-2018.

PEW RESEARCH CENTER

5. Trump on Immigration: "A Vicious Snake"

In National Harbor, Maryland at the Conservative Party Action Conference (CPAC) on February 23rd, 2018, President Donald Trump includes in his speech some remarks on immigration and illustrates them with a poem about a snake. He adds that you should replace the word snake by immigration.

See: https://www.youtube.com/watch?v=YXVt6z5INwM

In this poem, a vicious snake begs a tender-hearted woman "Take me in, oh tender woman", which the lady does. After the snake has regained forces, it bites the woman who dies.

The full text of President Donald Trump's speech – in which he also covers tax cuts, health care, the Second Amendment, gun control and armed teachers, trade deals and the stock market, the Dakota Access Pipelines, the Paris Climate Accord, Jerusalem as the capital of Israel, the Mexican wall, human trafficking and DACA – can be found here:

https://www.vox.com/policy-and-politics/2018/2/23/17044760/transcript-trump-cpac-speech-snake-mccain

Post-viewing Activities and Exam Preparation

Worksheet   **Dealing with Trauma of War**

10 credits content
15 credits language
Total: 25 credits

Tasks:

1. Briefly summarise what Lance Corporal Lu Lobello did in Baghdad in 2003.
2. How does the military psychiatrist explain psychological trauma? What should happen during the soldiers' preparation for combat?
3. What does Lu Lobello do to overcome his trauma?
4. Point out what Walt Kowalski does to atone for what he did in Korea.

Extract: **Atonement**

Dexter Filkins, The New Yorker, Oct. 29th and Nov. 5th 2012

Jonathan Shay, a psychiatrist who has advised the military on psychological trauma, told me that some of the most severely affected soldiers suffer "moral injury". "It occurs when you've done something in the moment that you were told by your superiors that you had to do, and believed, truthfully and honourably, that you had to do, but which nonetheless violated your own ethical commitments," he said. "It's bad moral luck. Unfortunately, war is filled with that." Typical soldiers, Shay told me, do not regard themselves as murderers. "There is a bright line between murder and legitimate killing that means everything to them," he said. "Any civilian who says that in war there are no rules – that's bullshit." The rules of engagement are central to soldiers' well-being. "They hate it when they have killed somebody they didn't need to kill. It's a scar on their soul."

Lance Corporal Lu Lobello, 22, machine gunner in Fox Company's 3rd Platoon talks about April 16, 2003 in Baghdad. He is armed with an M-249 machine gun which fires a thousand rounds a minute.

The marines on Baladiyat (eastern Baghdad) appear to have followed the rules they were given. But at one point Lobello suggested that the rules were far too loose. "What bothers me is that, by the time we got set up and consolidated, the understanding was: if they drive down the street, that's it – it doesn't matter, just fucking shoot them," Lobello said. "But we didn't have one single suicide bomber. And these guys that were running at our position – were they? Were they really? Or did we just shoot them while they were driving toward us?"

Lobello had only the vaguest idea how many Iraqis they had killed and wounded; he could remember only the frenzy of it, the terrifying thrill, the streams of bullets going in. "A lot of times, I think what happened was, somebody would realize, Fuck, dude, we're not shooting the right people. But it was like the beast was already going. You can't say hold on, stop, wait – no way."

In a Mercedes that came towards them, he shot at a family, killing the father and two sons. They were on their way home and waved a white flag.

After he was discharged three years later, he started to look for them with the help of the reporter. He hoped that when he had talked to them he would find rest and sleep again.

(https://www.newyorker.com/magazine/2012/10/29/atonement)

For the teacher:

1. When Lance Corporal Lu Lobello was 22, he fought in Baghad as a gunner in the 3rd Platoon. He was armed with a machine gun which fires a thousand rounds per minute. Their orders were to shoot at all Iraquis coming towards them. He remembers firing an endless stream of bullets; and he is not able to forget the family in their Mercedes who drove towards them waving a white flag. He shot the father and two sons.

2. The military psychiatrist explains that trauma is caused when a person has killed somebody that they needn't kill. It does not matter if there was an order by the soldier's superiors; the soldier's personal moral integrity is violated and he experiences it as a scar on his soul.

3. Lu Lobello has enlisted a reporter with whose help he wants to find the surviving members of the family he shot in Baghdad in 2003. He wants to talk to them as a way of dealing with his guilt.

4. In Korea, Walt and the others stormed a snipers' nest. With his machine gun he shot a young Korean who was about to hand himself in.

After he has befriended young Thao and helped him find a job, Walt feels responsible for Thao's safety now and in the future. That is why he confronts the leader of the Hmong gang, Smokie; he beats him up and threatens him. This starts a spiral of violence as the gang retaliate by shooting at the Lors' home and by raping Sue.

Now Walt not only has the young Korean on his soul, but also the horrible attack on Sue.
Walt knows that he suffers from a serious illness and decides to make sure that Sue and Thao can live without the gang's interference. He confronts the gang unarmed and provokes them with insults. He waits until many neighbours witness the scene. He pulls out his lighter deliberately fast and, while murmuring "Hail Mary full of grace", he is pierced by bullets. In a bird's eye shot, we see him lying on his back, both arms stretched out, like Jesus on the cross.
Walt has sacrificed himself to atone for his sins.

* * *

Further Task:

Find out more about the My Lai court-martials (for example from http://famous-trials.com/mylaicourts) and explain this statement:

The military is based on a strong sense of duty to follow orders. Emphasis should be taken away from following orders blindly and encourage soldiers and commanding officers to individually evaluate orders handed down to them. War is a time of high emotion, and often does not allow for time to ponder moral values. Moral actions should be engrained in a soldier before they are sent into combat. As a world leader the U.S. needs to hold very high standards for their own men, to provide an example and encourage abidance of the law of war.

(Statement made after the My Lai court-martials)

For the teacher:

The My Lai court-martials deal with two tragic events during the American involvement in Viet Nam. One is the massacre by U.S. soldiers of as many as 500 unarmed civilians – old men, women and children – in My Lai on March 16, 1968. The other is the cover-up of that massacre.

Post-viewing Activities and Exam Preparation

Worksheet   Everyday Racism – A Personal Statement

Tasks:

1. Sum up Michael Wong's text about himself.
2. Why does he quote the sentence from MLK's "I Have a Dream" speech?
3. How does he define racism? Why does he oppose politically correct hyphenated terms?
4. Discuss: Demonstrating one's racial sensitivity by "respecting these various cultures" is racist.

Encountering Everyday Racism

As a member of a visible minority, and one partner in an interracial marriage, I think I have some grounds on which to speak of the issue of racism. Just as you cannot understand love until you've experienced it, you cannot understand racism until you've experienced it first-hand. Unfortunately, I understand racism all too well.

Just below my hairline on the left side, I still bear a scar from a vicious schoolyard racial attack I suffered as a child, at the hands of an adolescent. He wasn't even *suspended* for trying to bludgeon a small child with a brick, because (as a white teacher explained) he came from a "broken home", which somehow made his behaviour acceptable. The crime was swept under the carpet, but the scar remains. Like an angry white line, it reminds me of the meaning of hate every time I look into a mirror. And in my heart, I still bear scars from many other racist attacks I 've suffered throughout my life, including racial slurs from all manner of people and repeated accusations from my wife's German Mennonite relatives that our interracial marriage was "against the will of God". These scars are the reason that I am furious when people who have never suffered from racism try to downplay it, or redefine it to suit their purposes.

"I have a dream that my four little children will one day live in a nation where they will not be judged by the color of their skin, but by the content of their character." Martin Luther King, Jr., August 28, 1963

The Definition of Racism

What is racism? If we simply examine the structure of the word, it would appear obvious that the word "racism" should be interpreted just like all the other "isms". Just as humanism upholds the importance of human rights, nationalism upholds the importance of national differences, and theism upholds the importance of divine beings, racism upholds the importance of race.

Does race matter? In an ideal world, it wouldn't. The fact that I am of Asian descent shouldn't mean anything to anyone, on any grounds, except as a point of purely academic trivia. But that's an ideal world. In the real world, have we been moving toward this ideal, or away from it? Does the "political correctness" movement help, or hurt?

I feel that modern political correctness, far from reducing racism, is actually *increasing* it. One example is the politically correct terminology for visible minorities. In America, people of African descent are referred to as "African-Americans". People of Asian descent are referred to as "Asian-Americans". People of Indian descent are referred to as "Indian-Americans". Some of these terms are championed by members of those races, but I *strongly* object to them. If a young black man traces his American lineage back for ten generations, grows up in Detroit and never sees Africa, why should he be referred to as an "African-American"? Doesn't that imply that he's half-African, and half-American? Why isn't he *all* American? Why aren't the descendants of European settlers referred to as "Anglo-Americans", or

"Aryan-Americans"? When I hear one of these hyphenated race names, it implies to me that the person has recently immigrated from Africa, or India, or Asia. Therefore, I see no justification whatsoever to apply such terms to people whose grandparents were born here. It accentuates the differences, and implies that they are "imports", rather than a natural part of the local culture.

The politically correct media is constantly reminding us of the distinction between the alien cultures of non-whites and the presumably domestic culture of whites. The television is awash in documentaries and soundbites about "Black culture" or "Asian culture" or "Latino culture", and people proudly demonstrate their "racial sensitivity" by "respecting" these various "cultures". What a crock! This show of "respect" is *completely* racist, no matter what the politically correct brigade may say. To even describe something called "Asian culture" is to subtly make two claims:
1. All people descended from Asian immigrants act the same.
2. People of Asian descent have different cultural values than "we" do.

The same is true whenever someone talks about "Black culture" or "Latino culture". The none-too-subtle implication is that members of visible minorities have conflicting cultural and national loyalties, torn between here and their "homelands". To put it another way, why don't we ever hear about "white culture"? No one talks about "white culture" because everyone knows two things:
1. There are many different types of "white" culture. The British, French, Irish, Italians, Germans, Russians, etc. are much different from one another.
2. Once people have been here for more than a generation or two, we should assume that they've adjusted to local cultural values.

Why don't we make those same assumptions about people who *aren't* white? Are we supposed to perpetuate the notion that all Asians act the same, or all Blacks act the same? Are we supposed to promote the notion that members of visible minorities are incapable of accepting local cultural values, or that they have some unbreakable spiritual connection to the birthplace of their ancestors which will forever separate them from white people?

Oh, I know, the politically correct brigade might point out that white people aren't the only ones who talk about "Black culture" or "Asian culture". Well, that doesn't prove anything. No one ever said that white people are the only racists in the world, so you can't prove that an act isn't racist by showing that a non-white person does it. I've seen black people accuse other black people of "not acting black enough", and I've seen Asians accuse other Asians of "being yellow on the outside and white on the inside". It's truly disgusting to me that a member of a visible minority can actually be criticized for not conforming to racial stereotypes.

So, if you want to be racially sensitive, don't bullshit me about your great respect and admiration for "Asian culture". Asian culture does not exist. I don't know of any such thing. People from Japan, Korea, Indonesia, and China have markedly different cultural values, and people from different regions or different social groups within those countries also have markedly different cultural values. As for me, I don't belong to any of those groups. I love burgers and pizza. I watch NFL football on TV. I only speak English. I drive a Mercury. My dog is a family pet, not a snack. And when someone asks me whether I'm Chinese or Japanese, I tell him I'm neither. I'm a Canadian. End of story.

Essay reproduced with the kind permission of Michael Wong, 2010